"We trained hard, but it seemed that every time we were beginning to form up into teams, we would be reorganized. I was to learn later in life that we tend to meet any new situation by reorganizing; and a wonderful method it can be for creating the illusion of progress while producing confusion, inefficiency, and demoralization."
. . . Gaius Petronius Arbiter, Roman Satirist, 210 BC.

While likely a false citation, it is at least known to have been said much later by Charlton Ogburn, Jr. (1911-1998).

It is not important who first uttered this cogent thought. When a business is not organized in such a way as to allow you to work efficiently and effectively, it has failed to make working what it should be. At the same time, when you don't clearly know what your work is, how to improve it, and how to work as an individual and within a team, both you and the business suffer. This book is designed to help you and the organization understand how to achieve optimal work and continuous improvement.

Danny Langdon
Originator of the Language of Work™
Business Consultant, 2018

THE
BUSINESS
MODEL

FOR EXECUTIVES

THE
BUSINESS
MODEL

USING THE LANGUAGE OF WORK
TO ORGANIZE AND ALIGN WORK

BOOK 1 OF THE WORK TRILOGY

DANNY G. LANGDON
KATHLEEN S. LANGDON

© 2018 Performance International

Published by:
Performance International
5 Oval Court
Bellingham, WA 98229 USA
360-738-4010
www.performanceinternational.com
info@performanceinternational.com

Although the author and publisher have made every effort to ensure that the information in this book was correct at press time, the author and publisher do not assume and hereby disclaim any liability to any party for any loss, damage, or disruption caused by errors or omissions, whether such errors or omissions result from negligence, accident, or any other cause. The advice and contents in this book are the author's opinion. The author is not making any claims or promises, and if you would like to put anything into action, please consult a business professional.

ISBN Paperback: 978-0-9913975-7-0
ISBN eBook: 978-0-9913975-4-9

The Language of Work™

The Language of Work™ (LoW) is a systemic, enterprise-wide system for organizing, managing, implementing, and continuously improving work by means of powerful integration tools. This goal is achieved through the universal use of a Work Formula that is applied through a process known as Work Analytics to a series of integrated Work Implementation Models. While that sentence is a mouthful, this book turns it into a series of easily understood, illustrated pieces.

The anchor of the Language of Work is the Work Formula: a behaviorally based, clear reflection of work using a standard formula to apply various Work Analytic Tools. Its use allows:

- executive management to provide everyone with a shared understanding of the business mission, ultimate goals, and ongoing objectives;
- managers to effectively facilitate employee achievement; and
- workers to do their parts individually and in teams by thoroughly understanding work and committing to its continuous improvement and overall implementation.

Every business consists of people and jobs at all levels of the organization. Communication within and between these levels is paramount to business success. The three Work Implementation Models of the LoW are an excellent method of addressing this basic quality of business. A separate book is devoted to each one:

The Business Model

Primarily for executives, this book demonstrates how to organize a business to achieve work alignment, operational transparency, and continuous improvement. The model applies to all four levels where work is planned and accomplished. Ways to align organizational needs related to standards, work support, human relations, and financial support are also provided. The book is also recommended reading for managers and workers who want a complete understanding of the Language of Work as it relates their role in the business as a whole.

The Managing Model

Primarily for managers, including team leaders, this book explains how the Language of Work, through Work Analytic Tools, can facilitate various management functions to achieve continuous work improvements. The Managing Model is a logical, systemic extension of The Business Model. Thus, what the executive develops through The Business Model managers can effectively facilitate using the same Work Formula. The book will also be of interest to workers aspiring to a managerial role.

The Working Model

Primarily for workers, this book shows how to use the Language of Work Formula to implement and continuously improve work as an individual worker and as part of a team. Using a variety of Work

Analytic Tools, individuals and teams can work together to meet executive and management work goals. Using the Work Formula they learn how to continuously improve work to maximize work effectiveness, efficiency, and to effect needed changes as they are planned by management. Managers will want to read this book to support their facilitation of work.

Each of the three books in *The Work Trilogy* is written for a specific audience; each is independent, and yet all three comprise an integrated system. To make each book stand alone, a certain amount of redundancy is needed. We trust the reader of two or all three of the books will not find this bothersome. As with any new language, the Language of Work demands practice and repetition. Deeper insights can occur as one reads again, learning the many nuances of this new way to look at and practice the work of business.

As you learn new ways, the authors hope you will share that knowledge with us, and we welcome questions as you use the Language of Work.

Danny and Kathleen Langdon

The Business Model: A Book for Executive Management

This book was written to reach management at all levels of an enterprise, but especially executives responsible for defining and organizing the what and how of the business. It will introduce you to a way of organizing the business so as to achieve needed work alignment to the business goals and to establish transparency for universal understanding. It will also provide an effective way to achieve continuous improvement (and introduce painlessly any changes you may need as the environment shifts and the enterprise grows). The book will show you a systematic approach that has been proven to work and can for your enterprise.

This book is written with just enough detail to demonstrate the importance and value of a new way of organizing and aligning work. Its application should result in a well-honed organization in which everyone understands better what they and others do for the value of customers and clients. When combined with the other two books of *The Work Trilogy*, you and your supervisory personnel and workers will all be on the same page of a shared understanding to manage, implement, and continually improve the work of the enterprise.

Danny Langdon
Originator of the Language of Work
Performance International
5 Oval Court, Bellingham, WA 98229
www.performanceinternational.com

Contents

Acknowledgements

Thanks to several executives representative of those for whom we wrote the book. Their ideas and suggestions were very instrumental in keeping the book centered on your needs and circumstances. Thanks to Roby James, our copyeditor, for helping us to communicate effectively our Language of Work. Thanks to Brittney Langdon for final proofing.

And special thanks to our "third-party" readers—Joanna Berg, Meg Lang, and Brenda Sample—who worked so diligently to find any last minute, glaring illustration or reading issues. Very special thanks to Ghislain Viau, Creative Publishing Book Design for working with us on cover designs, print and eBook formatting. With so many at-the-last minute edits and changes on three books at the same time he was very patient and extremely professional.

Danny and Kathleen Langdon

Preface

Everyone has their own perception of the work of an organization, and that is precisely the problem with work. One sees it by the org chart, others by function, or by the jobs and teams, and still others by the processes. Or worse yet, we only see the enterprise in terms of what we do. It's time for a common way to view business, understand how to improve it where needed, manage and do our work in concert with that shared understanding. That is where the Language of Work comes into play.

While we were writing this book, we often had conversations with a wide range of friends, colleagues and clients, who inquired about the subject of the book as part of the Trilogy of Work. As soon as we revealed the working title and basic content, the universal response was a not-so-unexpected, "Boy! Could my current (or former) company or department use this kind of systematic approach to understanding and organizing business!" Nearly everyone thinks businesses could be run better; they also agree that organizations are rarely defined and understood well. We have helped facilitate several organizations using the LoW and confirmed that it works. It will work for you!

Danny and Kathleen Langdon

Chapter 1

How We Think Work Is Organized and Why That Needs To Change

We begin with a fundamental question: *How do you personally see the work of your business?*

If you have ever been involved in the formation of a business or its reorganization, you likely see work in a particular way. That's because you are forced, with others, to initiate or rethink how things are done. What, for instance, is it that needs to change organizationally or to be done in a certain way? Division of labor, for example, is perhaps the most common way to view the work in an organization. That is in large part why executives play with organization charts. But if you had the opportunity to view and structure work other ways, what would that be? Is it, as another way, a series of goals, objectives, and strategies and plans to be met? Is it some series of jobs to be done? Is it specific processes to be

> Everyone has their own view of what a business is and how it is best organized and operated. We ask that you set your view aside for the moment and consider that there is a better way to organize, manage, and work within a business.

followed? Does work take a team or matrix management approach? Are you one of those executives who drive everything financially? In the final analysis is it just easier to have some "division of labor" that is manifested in a traditional organization chart? And finally, if all else fails, is the work a combination of these approaches to work that will somehow surely integrate the work of many into one unified business? Furthermore, will everyone understand the work and implement it for the common mission, vision, strategies, goals, and objectives?

The first thing to accept is that businesses do not generally know how to organize enterprises efficiently or effectively. That may be hard to accept as an executive, but doing so will open up the possibility to a way that is much more effective. Most organizations grow up in a mismatch of what seems necessary. In other words, someone has a great idea for a business, they ally with others, hire for various positions as they deem needed, organize these into groups generally based on commonality of work, and support them to achieve their goals and objectives as best they think. This may even work at times, but it hardly is a systematic path to organization and implementation, nor an alignment of the work such that everyone is truly working for the common ends. There has got to be a better way. And now there is.

We will introduce a very systematic, easy-to-understand and use Business Model utilizing what is known as the Language of Work. Now over 25 years in the making, refinement, and successful use in many businesses, this systemic approach to organization has been proven to work. It clearly delineates and aligns all the various levels and layers of work, from top to bottom and laterally in the company. Then, in other implementation models of work, we reveal how best to manage and how best to be a worker.

If that wasn't enough, we add an important bonus. The Language of Work will more easily allow you to make the ongoing, continuous changes that are inevitable in today's rapidly changing business environments.

Chapter 2

What Are the Desired Characteristics of a Well-Organized Business?

The paramount reason to organize is to assure that everything in the enterprise works together—is in alignment. You want the organization to achieve business goals using defined strategies, by people who explicitly know their work and are well-managed or self-driven. Anything less will be a waste of time and resources and is unlikely to maximize efficiency or effectiveness.

Organizing the right way from the start, especially in the case of a new enterprise, is rare. Instead, businesses tend to start and grow spontaneously and in a highly reactive mode. Once established, the enterprise finds that new technology or other business needs emerge, demanding that processes and organization change.

The re/organization of a business has often been limited to changes in the org. chart for making work improvements. This chapter emphasizes the value of achieving work alignment, transparency and assuring continuous improvement as necessary to overall organizational effectiveness and efficiency.

More production is needed, so additional resources are added; nobody seems to be managing this or that function, so someone is put in charge. A new product line or support task is added—not necessarily planned in relation to already existing functions. The number of employees expands, and everyone's feeling of knowing what's going on or being valued diminishes. Perks, processes or people are eliminated without regard to their impact on those left in place. Expectations grow, and tensions mount. Skilled, highly experienced people leave; they are replaced with new, usually less experienced ones, accustomed to different, possibly ill-fitting procedures, costing productivity and client satisfaction. The worker pool ages, and their experience and knowledge are not captured to assure ongoing success. Management gets distant. The culture begins to "smell." If the business had been well-organized from the beginning, it would have had the resilience to accommodate major and minor changes. By its very intent, work reorganization tries to solve these problems and create an organization that works more efficiently. Next thing you know, it's time to reorganize again. But such tweaks will not generally work, because there are simply too many problems to solve, nor will they create a true understanding of how to actualize needed improvements. Getting organized systematically is the answer.

Being organized the right way should achieve three organizational needs:

> *Alignment*
> *Transparency*
> *Continuous Improvement*

These three needs can be achieved using a single, repeatable, systematic process in which the goals are considered equal and consistent with one another at every level and layer of the business. Otherwise, they cause separately programmed approaches and are weakened because the organization is approached in piecemeal fashion.

This chapter is a succinct introduction to alignment, transparency, and continuous improvement as they relate to organization of an enterprise—what we will call here, "The Business Model." The remaining chapters will describe how these paramount organizational needs can be achieved together using one simple formula for work.

Alignment

Traditionally, alignment has referred to making sure that goals, strategies and tactics build on one another. This is obviously necessary to overall enterprise success. But an additional kind of alignment is needed as well. Alignment, as used here, relates much more to work execution within and between various levels (i.e., jobs and processes) in the organization. Following this work execution alignment, there is then an alignment needed with standards, work support, human relations and financial considerations. At its very core, alignment is everything that can be thought of as "the work." Fundamentally, the work alignment includes interrelating and coordinating:

WHAT the business is/wants to be as an enterprise; with

HOW the work is or will be done; with

WHO is performing or will perform the work;

in a matrix of what the **WORK GROUPS** would be and how to **MANAGE** them,

to desired **STANDARDS** to be achieved, through

WORK SUPPORT by a "healthy culture" in which the culture can be optimized, which

accounts for **HUMAN RELATIONS** issues that might get in the way of work, the general tenor of the work environment, and customer relations, and finally

sufficient **FINANCIAL SUPPORT** to assure that work is optimally possible.

That is obviously, a mouthful, so we will break it down and link all of this systemically since they all influence one another.

The first four, WHAT, HOW, WHO, and WORK GROUPS/ MANAGEMENT, are identified in the Business Model as the "levels" of work. Collectively, these four are also known as Work Execution. Then, related to Work Execution are four "layers" of work that also need alignment. Thus, all Work Execution needs to meet certain STANDARDS, have adequate WORK SUPPORT, is influenced by HUMAN RELATIONS, and finally all work needs certain FINANCIAL SUPPORT. Thus, the four levels and four layers must be aligned with one another. The only way to achieve this is with a formula of work that defines (or what we call models) work in the same way (the Work Formula). This will make all aspects of work understandable to everyone in the enterprise through the Language of Work.

Additionally, with the same formula of work being used, transparency will naturally exist, since every aspect of work will be clear to everyone, and change or continuous improvement will regularly, systematically, and systemically occur using the same Work Formula. Again, a mouthful to digest, but we will continue to break it all down and show how all levels and layers can work together.

Transparency

The second reason to get organized using a commonly applied Work Formula is the need for transparency in the enterprise. Transparency is a relatively new concept for business, because business has traditionally been viewed as a hierarchical structure in which the executive management and others supposedly know everything and the workers just do as they're told. Such a view still persists in some measure in many businesses, but it is gradually changing through the introduction of such concepts as teamwork, Six Sigma, participative management, certain innovations in computer "dashboard software" to plan and track work, and the like.

> "What can be done to attain alignment, transparency, and continuous improvement so that the means for getting organized and doing work encompasses all three?"

"Transparency" refers to the extent that everyone unambiguously understands what is going on in the company *operationally* relative to business intent. At the lowest rank, transparency tells the employees how well their department is doing and what their specific contribution is. Transparency also tells the various work groups their exact relationship and how their work output is another's work input. Transparency expands to the knowledge of how well everything in the business is being done, and how each worker can contribute to making anything else in the company better without fear of reprisal or being told "it's none of your business!"

It is not just protection of power bases that can limit the efficiency of business operations by the lack of true transparency. There is often also a lack of transparency because, to date, there hasn't been a structured way for everyone to look at work communally, a common model of work that defines the business operationally (at every level and layer), allowing everyone to understand and identify problems and solutions together. The Language of Work will make it possible to realize true transparency of work, and in a truly transparent business, everyone knows what everyone else knows. Thus, anyone can help to make the business better.

Continuous Improvement

Finally, in achieving the ultimately well-organized enterprise, continuous improvement has recently been recognized as a necessity. This is primarily because today's business needs to change rapidly to meet changes in competition and the marketplace. How to achieve that continuous improvement has mostly taken the form of add-on institutionalized programs (e.g., Total Quality Program Initiatives, Six Sigma) or programs such as process reengineering and Lean Manufacturing. However, as useful as these have proven themselves individually, they are not typically integrated with alignment and transparency as a permanent part of the ongoing work system. This is a problem that the Work Formula solves.

The three qualities—alignment, transparency, and continuous improvement—are not separate functions in a well-run enterprise. Rather, the three should be fully integrated and ongoing.

The question to ask about getting better organized is simple:

"What can be done to attain alignment, transparency and continuous improvement so that the means for getting organized, being managed, and doing work encompasses all three?"

Successfully answering this question will mean that numerous full-blown, disruptive reorganizations are rarely needed again. The enterprise will be continuously organized for maximum effectiveness and efficiency as it does its work. It will not need a program or piecemeal approach to work improvement.

Chapter 3

What Are the Essential Elements of a Systems Approach to Getting Business Aligned?

To be effective—and to avoid the failures associated with not achieving work alignment—management must use a systems approach to its business model. The essential elements of a systems approach incorporate the following:

1—Work as a Systemic System

Unlike how most people see work today, a systemic view of work recognizes that there are basic elements of business behavior. These elements produce work and must be taken into

A systematic, proven way to organize will assure success. Here you will be introduced to the essential elements that comprise a systems approach as a prelude to the introduction of the Language of Work.

account if the business is to be maximized. Employing a specific and optimum order of analysis is critical to effective organization. The process systemically ties together the different elements of the business. Work is seen as behavior, not simply as tasks and assignments. Work is not just goals, but operationally how they are achieved. And, if you fix one part of the business, how will that affect other levels and layers? Once real clarity about work exists, objective decisions can be made regarding the organizational structure that will best enable the enterprise to succeed.

In broad terms, the process you are about to be introduced to is an alignment of the levels and layers introduced in Chapter 2: levels WHAT, HOW, WHO, and ORGANIZATION, combined with different layers of work manifested in WORK STANDARDS, WORK SUPPORT, HUMAN RELATIONS, and FINANCIAL SUPPORT. This alignment process, with the assurance of executive sponsorship, results in a business well-designed to execute the work that achieves the desired enterprise goals.

This alignment process allows the organization to be explained and defended based on logic, rather than intuition or whim. It is devoid of politics or personal agendas or, at the minimum, makes such agendas so transparent as to minimize their negative influence. And employees have the information needed to accept the inevitable changes without emotion, trauma, resistance, or sabotage.

2—Continuous Improvement

The organization process should incorporate a way for built-in continuous improvement. Doing reorganizations time after time after time disrupts any enterprise. However, if the process incorporates repeatable and regularly planned organizational learning, making needed changes continuous, then you have a very powerful tool for keeping your enterprise evolving to meet changing needs. In other words, the organization process should teach people not only how to organize, but also how to continue to make improvements based on that system. Indeed, you will find that the system for organizing, using a Work Formula suggested here, will also be the very system for continually improving the work.

3—Clarification of Work

The organization process must be based on a definition or model that reflects, clarifies, and illuminates the work, both currently and in the future. The process should help to identify where the problems and opportunities for improvement are, while achieving agreement on priorities. Not surprisingly, organization is all about work. One of its by-products should be increased understanding by everyone in the enterprise of the exact nature of the goals, the jobs, the challenges required to accomplish these goals, and the ways in which executives can support the work effort.

4—Broad Understanding

The systemic process should ensure a broad understanding of the link between the organization's goals and the work that will accomplish those goals. This is to say that the process must be steeped in a behavioral, cause-and-effect relationship between what the enterprise wants to achieve and the tasks that will best accomplish those goals. As you will learn, this requires the understanding and use of a Work Formula applied to virtually every aspect of work—whether subtly applied through the systems-thinking that is learned by its continued use or directly as part of work when implemented (i.e. as in the solving of problems, review of another's performance, and so forth).

5—Employee Engagement

The process should capitalize on and channel employees' uncertainties and emotions, using them for productive, useful ends. To do so will require their proactive involvement in the organization process. There is no room for a "my way or the highway" approach if an effective organization is the desired outcome.

6—Objectivity

The process should be objective to eliminate personal executive agendas and politics. Nothing negates optimal work organization more thoroughly than a process which allows those in power to meet their personal needs and/or bias or agenda at great cost to others.

7—Employee Involvement

There are sound business reasons to assure transparency and employee involvement at every stage of organization and implementation. Employees should be involved in specific, guided ways that ensure their input is obtained, valued, and acted upon when it comes to virtually any aspect of a Business Model. They need to describe the current and future work to identify means that will improve, support, and implement that work. Besides, the more they are involved, the more they will be committed to success and change that is largely self-understood and driven.

8—Speed of Getting Organized and Improving

The process of getting organized and continuing to be better should take as little time as possible. Otherwise, the cost of achieving maximum work efficiency and effectiveness may well negate its economic value, while causing disruptions to work achievements and worker behavior. The process should therefore be quick and agile, with outcomes and follow-up visible to all.

Chapter 4

Introducing the Levels and Layers of the Business Model

Once an enterprise has identified what it wants to be as a business, then the organization or reorganization of that enterprise is primarily all about work. The answers to the following questions, in that order, will constitute what work needs to be known for modeling and alignment:

"**What** is the work?"

"**How** is the work to be executed?"

"**Who** will do the work?"

"What should the **work groups** be and how should they be **managed**?"

"What **standards** should the work rise to?"

The organization of a business would seem to be essentially about how the work is to be done. While this is the primary goal, the business must as well give careful attention to supporting work execution. This chapter introduces the eight major, interrelated levels and layers of organizing or reorganizing a business.

"How will the enterprise **support** work through a positive and healthy culture?"

"What **human relations** factors must be accounted for as to their impact on accomplishing work?" and

"What's the **financial support** that needs to exist to get work accomplished and be successful for the business?"

These eight questions will be abbreviated here, in order, as:

Levels:

> WHAT
>
> HOW
>
> WHO
>
> WORK GROUPS and MANAGEMENT

Layers:

> WORK STANDARDS
>
> WORK SUPPORT
>
> HUMAN RELATIONS
>
> FINANCIAL SUPPORT

The ultimate goals are to reach work clarity and optimal work alignment. Each of these work levels and layers will be modeled in the above order because the answer to each forms the basis for those that follow. Also, there is a causal effect between these levels and layers that must be clearly understood to impact work in a positive direction. In this chapter you'll get a general introduction to the LoW Business Model. In a later chapter the Business Model will be illustrated through a sample business the authors previously helped organize for a mid-sized enterprise.

You will come to see that one of the most striking virtues of the eight levels and layers is that the tasks needed to accomplish each step can be completed in a reasonable time frame—weeks, not months. Because the decision-making is based on clear models of work involving almost everyone in the business, consensus, commitment to change and adjustments can be easily made. The current organization will not stop, stall, or lurch into reorganization after reorganization, but will smoothly flow toward maximizing work execution, creating desired results, and benefiting from a shared, understood approach. Or, if you are developing a new enterprise, you will quickly see how things can be achieved operationally and have a more accurate basis for the financing, development, and implementation requirements to get your business off the ground and running successfully.

The Business Model

The Way to Alignment, Transparency, and Continuous Improvement

The LoW Business Model is a logical path through the business that defines, describes, and models interrelated work to achieve desired business ends. The Business Model is illustrated in Figure 1. The explanation that follows will outline the eight key steps to aligning the work of a business. The chapters that follow will then illustrate through a sample business this systematic approach to work organization based on the Language of Work.

The Business Model

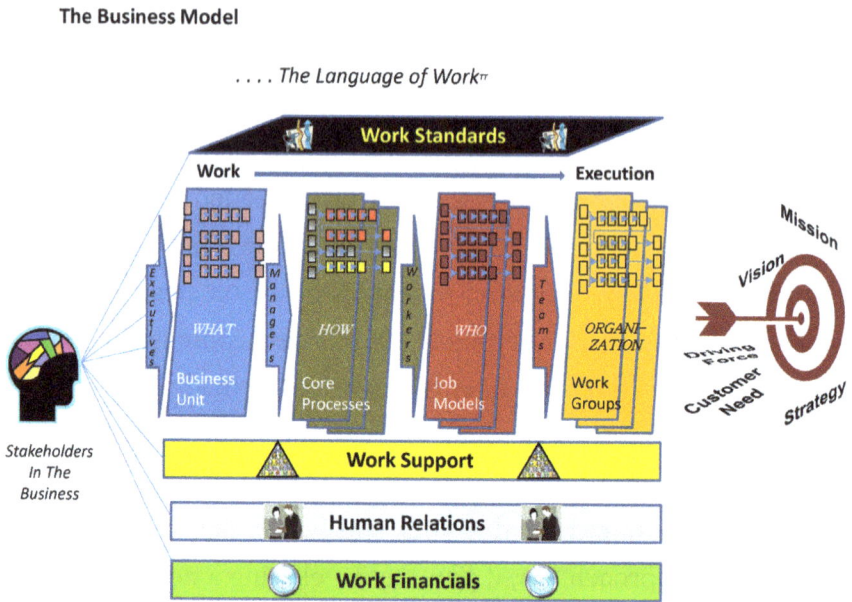

. . . . *The Language of Work*™

Figure 1

1—Addressing the WHAT of the Enterprise

Model: *The Business Unit*—(First Level of Work)

The success of any business depends on identifying the foundation the enterprise intends to rest on in its effort to achieve its intended mission/vision and goals.

WHAT does the organization want to be, and how will it distinguish itself, if desired, from others like it?

Many resources are available on goal-setting, determining vision/mission, developing strategic plans, determining the organization's driving force and competitive advantage, and other topics fundamental to the organization's identity. Perhaps no one has crystallized this better than James Collins, in his book *From Good to Great* (2001). The book is based on solid research regarding what constitutes success in both the profit and the nonprofit worlds. It also addresses how to distinguish your business from the competition and become not just good, but great. It's highly recommended reading from our point of view.

In our book we will not address the goals of business—those are yours to define. Rather, we are interested in how you define the best way, in terms of work execution, to achieve the business ends. The beginning point for this is the modeling of what we call the business unit—the first level of work.

As the foundation level of the eight-part Business Model, a business unit is an *operational* definition of WHAT the business is (now) or will be (in the future). It is what the executives (founders, partners, board of directors, owners, etc.) define at a high level their operational understanding of the business. This includes what the business is to achieve as outputs and consequences (more on this later), as well as how it works to achieve them organizationally. As with all the levels and layers of work, we will be using the Language of Work Formula (introduced in the next chapter) to define and establish shared consensus of the all levels and layers of the Business Model—at the level by and for the senior management.

In our consulting practice we use an analogy of American football to illustrate the various levels of a business. Thus, in professional football, the *business unit* is the franchise. The other levels include the playing of the game, sales, marketing, drafting,

23

etc. as *core processes*. The *jobs* are the actual roles of various players, coaches and support personnel. The *organization level* (of teams and management) is represented by the offense, defense, special teams, and who they are coached (managed) by. We will use this same analogy later when defining the work layers of standards, work support, human relations, and financial support.

Large corporations—the size of a Microsoft or a General Motors—have many business units and an overarching major business unit. For small businesses, the line between business unit and core processes can merge. The important question here is not the business size (because they can all be defined the same way with lesser or greater levels of complexity), but what the business wants to be to achieve its intended ends. Once it has defined what it is (present business) and/or what it wants to be (future business or desired state), it can then identify and describe how the core processes and other levels of jobs and teams/management will achieve the WHAT.

Business units, by the way, will be principally defined by executives and other key personnel who own and/or will be responsible for overall business success. We recommend use of a facilitator for this initial process. Use of a facilitator obviates the need for executives to lead the initial modeling effort, and it eliminates any tendencies they might have toward falling back on previously established policies or prejudices about work. Furthermore, a facilitator provides the objectivity to speed a more neutral and consensus building modeling process and outcome.

2—Addressing HOW Work Will Be Done

Model: *The Core Processes*—(Second Level of Work)

Basically, the missing ingredient for successfully organizing an enterprise has always been a way to define and align the core processes with an understanding of the business unit on the front end and on the back end with jobs and teams/management that will accomplish the work. Alignment is not achieved solely by carefully linking goals and objectives with well-defined strategies. Alignment for work execution can only be achieved by the use of a work behavioral model that accurately reflects how work is done in the business at various levels and layers. You will soon learn that this alignment is best achieved by the use of the Language of Work Formula, which creates a very operational approach.

The question here is: How is the business going to accomplish what it wants to accomplish? How are the "ops" folks going to operationally define how they want things done, and will this be consistent with what the executives want? Executives tend to understand the organization at the business unit level. So long as organizations are conducted without a systematic process for integrating the WHAT of executive

> So long as organizations are conducted without a systematic process for integrating the WHAT of executive knowledge with the HOW of operations, the WHO of workers/jobs and WORK GROUPS/ MANAGEMENT successful alignment will not be achieved.

knowledge with the HOW of operations, the WHO of workers/ jobs with the WORK GROUPS and MANAGEMENT, successful alignment will not be achieved, and the organization is likely to fail, or certainly be highly inefficient and/or ineffective.

Once we have successfully aligned the WHAT (the business unit level) with the HOW (the core processes level), we can then align individual jobs to these two levels so that they work in concert with one another.

3—Addressing the WHO of Work
Model: *The Jobs*—(Third Level of Work)

We have consistently found that individual employees know their own work well. However, intrinsically knowing the job and communicating it to others is not the same, especially when it comes to the information needed to achieve work alignment. But because such information is crucial, businesses need a better way to define individual work—jobs—to align them to core processes. Current means like job descriptions do not suffice. Nor does relying on the most current ways of defining core processes (e.g., so-called, "swim lanes"). They fail to adequately communicate intended individual job and team tasks in executing the core processes. SAP installation has been a prime example of this failure to link jobs to core processes.

Individual jobs arise in most businesses in a generally haphazard manner. Businesses have identified work that must be accomplished, so they hire someone with what they believe is the right background, experience, personality, and drive to do that work.

Or they provide formal orientation and training in various forms to fill in the skills required for the execution of jobs. Or they rely on on-the-job training to meet the need. Job titles and so-called job descriptions often drive what is sought in hiring workers, along with judgment about perceived job requirements.

This is pretty much to say that jobs are filled without much real regard for the core processes they are to execute. Processes are defined one way—or not at all—and jobs are defined another. Thus there can be little real operational alignment between core processes and jobs, just as between the business unit and the core processes.

Consequently, a business ends up with workers who are confused to varying degrees as to the value of their work, unhappy with what they do, missing some of the skills needed, or unable to identify and communicate with others how to make their jobs better fit with the overall enterprise. Even managers may not know exactly what their workers are or should be doing. Inefficiency abounds. Gossip and "politics" are rife. People who understand their work and how they fit into the enterprise's strategic mission have neither time nor patience for pettiness.

There is a way to better understand and improve your own work, and to make it function in operational alignment with core processes and the business unit. When this is done, managers are better able to manage those who work under them. This better way is called *job modeling*, and it is a key element in organizing and aligning business work.

4—Addressing the WORK GROUPS
Model: *Teams*—(Fourth Level of Work)

Just as jobs must be aligned with core processes, which must in turn be aligned with business units, teams must be aligned with the jobs, core processes, and business unit as well. That requires an operational model of work we call the Language of Work Formula.

A team should be a group of jobs with a set of common outputs and consequences facilitated by its managers/team leaders. In instances where the business choses to have self-directed teams, it speaks even more so that such teams explicitly know their work relative to and be aligned to the core processes. Teams, or work groups, in large part determine what the organizational structure will be.

Once the teams or work groups are defined, we can identify and further define the management positions they will need to help facilitate the work. As a corollary need, identifying and developing the organization chart would then be relatively easy, since we know precisely and have aligned the elements of an organization. The org chart is best revealed and structured at the end of this fourth level—not the beginning as is most often done in traditional organizing or reorganization of a business.

5—Defining Needed Work Standards
Matrix: Quality, Quantity, Timeliness, and Cost— (First Layer of Work)

In the fifth phase of the Business Model, we address the level of standards to which work should be expected to rise. Work is, after all, not just a matter of completion, but meeting goals or exceeding expectations, especially as it regards customer satisfaction and continuation of the business as an entity. The layer, of work known as Work Standards should be a systematic approach to assuring that standards are set when and where needed, rather than by a typically random act according to individual choice and/or mandated by outside entities.

Standards are the level of excellence that makes execution acceptable to business, professional, and/or personal needs and growth. If the work of a football player is defined by a job model of his position on the field, then an expectation for his performance (e.g., how many sacks he makes in a season) is one standard by which his playing can be measured. The same is true of other workers, teams, processes, and the overall business expectations.

In the Language of Work, standards are one of the four major layers of work, along with work support, human relations, and financial support. The key is knowing where and in what form standards should be set; to do so requires a way commensurate with the definition of work execution. A job aid for setting standards will be introduced to you for this purpose and will prove most effective in a thorough analysis of what standards need to be specified. This Work Standards Matrix will provide guidance in setting standards related to quantity, quality, timeliness, and cost, as these are the generally accepted classes of standards in business.

Additional details will be provided when we show an example of a business organized in the Business Model of the Language of Work (Chapter 5). For now, it will be helpful for you to think about the current standards in your business. Later we will suggest others based on the LoW Standards Matrix.

6—Addressing Work Support
Matrix: *The Culture*—(Second Layer of Work)

In the sixth phase we come to what may be, for many, a never-before-considered aspect of organizing a business. It's the notion of organizing all aspects of the culture of a business to support the expected work execution. That is why we refer to this important layer of work as Work Support.

Understanding, improving, and organizing for work execution is vital, since it most directly achieves the business goals. As already repeatedly noted, it is critical to first align work execution through definition of the four levels of work: from the business unit (WHAT), then to well-defined and understood core processes (HOW), through individuals who do the jobs (WHO) and through the WORK GROUPS. This alignment allows everyone to work together and be well-managed by those in charge.

However, think for a moment about competitive swimmers (in individual events, in relays, or as part of a synchronized team). They need water quality that allows optimal performance: not too hot or too cold, not polluted. The Summer Olympics swimming events are always in the most technologically clean and constructed facilities, so as to make possible maximum performance. Just as great swimmers cannot perform as well in polluted water, every business needs to operate in a healthy work environment. We describe this healthy environment as one which provides and ensures organizational support for work execution. Without a healthy work environment, lost productivity wastes time and resources, and much worker angst can occur. The more granular description that follows of how to clearly define the culture of an organization so that it is aligned to the work execution will help you see the power of linking work support to work execution at the four levels of work.

A variety of work support factors must be accounted for to foster a healthy culture. Generally, these factors have been addressed in most companies in separate, random ways. Some of these are summarized in Figure 2:

Work Need	Organizational Support Intervention
How is the work defined for each person?	Job Description
How will job performance be evaluated?	Performance Review Form
How will client satisfaction be determined?	Client Survey
How will process be changed?	Process Reengineering
What are my benefits?	Policies & Procedures Manual
How do I improve myself?	Training Programs
How do I get introduced to the company?	Orientation Program
How do I relate to my boss?	Management Practices

Figure 2

Work support is usually provided by the enterprise primarily as a series of unrelated organizational interventions, processes, practices, or programs like those shown above. In the development of the

Language of Work we identified nearly 120 different forms of work support. As an overview of work support, we will take a brief look at a few of these to show some ways to operationalize and align work using the Language of Work. We approach this by illustrating how work support influences each of the four levels of work execution.

Work Support for the Business Unit(s)

Can you picture a business not having a well-thought-out mission/vision statement, strategic plan, or set of goals and objectives? Imagine the impact their absence would have on work execution at the business unit level. Other needs at the business unit level include budgets, a decision/authority hierarchy, conditions, and regulations. Businesses may measure success with such items as client feedback, public relations, or business plans. Of course, all of these and others have effects as they support or fail to support the work of the business units. It is important to ask which elements of organizational support impact which aspects of work execution, and how. Not knowing the answers would potentially reduce efficiencies and effectiveness of work, as well as leaving unrecognized what to measure and improve.

Work Support for Core Processes

Once the core processes have been identified, a business needs to ensure that those core processes will be planned, implemented, and followed, while producing desired results. This involves determining the elements needed for the core processes to be optimally realized. These are elements such as capital equipment, raw materials, intellectual knowledge, the application of professional ethics and standards, automation, measurements and quality improvement of processes. An enterprise must know all the kinds of organizational support that affect core processes and identify which of them are most critical to success.

Work Support for Jobs

Although organizational support needs can suffer from the lack of consistent means and measurement of their cause-and-effect relation to work execution, at the job level they are generally well-known. For example, a worker's performance review is a typical means of job-level organizational support in most enterprises. It is the organizational provision for assessing one's job performance and determining what is being done well or needs improvement. Performance reviews are often used as well to identify training needs, other performance improvement opportunities, compensation adjustments, and future goal-setting.

> Approaching organizational support in a disjointed way, without regard to impact on work efficiency and effectiveness, is less than ideal.

There is a direct relationship between work execution (doing the work) and organizational support (seeing that work is done well). Thus, when a manager performs an accurate job review and improves individual performance, this is a means of organizational support. Unfortunately, while performance reviews are provided, few of these are presently effective; indeed, they are often described as worthless by employees.

In this case, organizational support at the individual job level is provided, but the organization does not maximize its use.

(Incidentally, there are ways to make performance reviews much better using the model we will introduce in Chapter 7.)

Another example of organizational support at the job level is the job description. Often the descriptions are not realistic and therefore are not helpful. Job descriptions should reflect what the expected work execution is to be, and they should be good enough to support other means of organizational support, such as performance reviews. This need for accuracy applies to many organizational support means, relating not only within a given level of work (e.g., job organizational support means), but between the levels of work (e.g., how a good job description relates to operationally achieving the business unit's mission/vision).

Work Support for Work Groups/Mgmt.
(Teams and Management)

Work Support related to work groups and management includes such elements as leadership practices, conflict resolution, management systems, partnership arrangements, and the like. As an example of cause and effect, conflict resolution, say, can have a much-needed positive impact on the work execution of teams, as well as that of individuals. When individuals or teams can't resolve long-standing issues with one another, productivity is negatively impacted; thus in this instance work support by the enterprise has failed. The same is true of any other means of work support.

How the various work support means are used, implemented, and improved in a business will not be a major focus of this book—other resources exist for this purpose. Rather, our focus is on their existence and alignment as part of an effective and efficient business model.

Approaching work support in a disjointed way, without regard to impact on work efficiency or effectiveness, is less than ideal. We often see businesses improving one or another means of work support without regard for its impact on other work support initiatives—or even on the work execution it is supposed to support. Isolated attention to just one or several means of work support can undercut any overall effort. If, for example, you mandate that every manager fill out a form that has been designed for a performance review, a filled-out form can become the goal, rather than an improved employee performance. Perhaps the form isn't even that good. Perhaps these reviews get in the way of daily execution of work, rather than building on that work execution as it is being done. Such an approach to improving performance is far too piecemeal and unlikely to achieve the results desired in support of work execution. We will show a convenient and useful way to collect work support data and constantly assure and improve such work support.

Thus, the focus of work support in this book is that it is to be systematically identified and provided in all its necessary dimensions as it relates to the organization of work execution on an ongoing basis. An alignment between work execution and work support is something that requires constant attention; otherwise the work execution suffers, and ultimately the business is harmed.

7—Addressing Human Relations

Matrix: *Making Sure People Cooperate And Are Treated Well*—(Third Layer of Work)

We all know that humans behave individually and do their own work in both positive and negative ways. We also have witnessed at its worst a possible profoundly negative effect on others and on the customer who doesn't return for our services or products. Knowing what's going on with employee behavior requires constant assessment of human relations; then doing things that mitigate negative behavior, while promoting desired individual and team behavior, requires more attention and remediation. As it does with work support and work standards, the LoW addresses the important role of attending to human relations and its effects on the entire business. We will be introducing you to a Human Relations Matrix that makes possible the alignment to Work Execution and identification of where and when improvement is needed.

8—Addressing Financial Support

Matrix: *Assuring Financial Means to Accomplish Work*—(Fourth Layer of Work)

Finally, we consider the importance of money. The position taken here is not so much the general issue of whether there is enough financial support as it is the particular influences upon the individual business. In the same way the LoW approaches the other layers of work, so too can financial considerations be planned and assessed on an on-going basis. Financial support takes the form of a useful matrix of needs that should be considered, tailored to your business situation, and continually assessed for adequacy in meeting business ends.

By way of summary then, the Business Model is a 6-4-4 (6 word work formula, 4 levels of work, and 4 layers of work) configuration for work alignment manifested through a formula for work behavior. For a summary of the 6-4-4 Business Model, and introduction to the Work Formula in the next chapter, you may want to access YouTube videos by the author explaining the work formula and the Business Model as a Business Optimization Dashboard (BOD):

https://youtu.be/Nn7tLm4nRLU

http://www.youtube.com/watch?v=WhS2KMdHm70

Chapter 5

The Language of Work Formula as a Systemic Approach to the Business Model

When employees, including executives, managers, workers, and team leaders, talk about, plan, implement, and suggest improvements, there can be many communication problems. In fact, communication problems at work are a major reason firms employ consultants. A common, mutually understood and useful way to discuss constructively what work is (except perhaps technically) and how to improve it did not exist until now. We might say that we were all singing, but without a musical score to follow.

> The Work Formula is introduced. The formula represents work behavior through six systemic elements. The Work Formula makes possible alignment, transparency and continuous improvement.

Lacking a formula, executives talk about goals, objectives, strategies, products, or services, while employees tend to talk about skills, knowledge, changes, activities, and problems. They are not on the same page. Watch at your next meeting to see if this is the case. You may observe this confusion when you are trying to solve an issue or find a better way to process work with any group.

Until now there has never been a universal "language of work" that centers communication, paints a clear picture of what work is composed of, and how the elements work (or don't work) together. No language has existed that allows discussion, promotes consensus, and facilitates clear understanding so as to eliminate subjective opinion while developing a shared objective knowledge of the work and how to improve it.

> To truly organize a business at any level requires a universally understood and applied way to operationally plan, relate and execute responsibilities, procedures and tasks across the entire workforce and management.

To truly organize a business for universal understanding requires a universally understood and applied way to operationally plan and execute responsibilities, procedures, and tasks across the entire workforce and management. Without it, organization, implementation, making improvements, and problem solving are left to guesswork, intuition, politics, personal agendas and posturing, leading to failure. Without a common understanding, work is a jumbled mess of who's responsible for what and cries of "Why don't they support what we do?" Each department of work is managed as if it were its own kingdom, without regard to the overall mission and vision that maximize profit and customer satisfaction.

Thus far, we have asked you to think of a business as four levels (business unit, core processes, jobs, and work groups/management), and four layers (work standards, work support, human relations, and financial support).

We will now introduce an easily understood and easily applied "Work Formula" of the Language of Work. This formula has six systemic elements that can be used to define and model each of the levels and layers of work. Using the same Work Formula for these allows us to align the levels and layers with one another and create greater understanding and clarity—transparency—up, down, and across the enterprise. The formula will also be a great aid in managing and continuous improvement.

Recognizing the need for a common definition, understanding, and alignment of work, we can now describe the Work Formula of the Language of Work and how it can be applied to actualize enterprises the best way.

A Work Formula Everyone Can Use Together

Enterprises, like the people who comprise them, exhibit behavior. Work behavior can be succinctly defined so that it is well understood by everyone in the company. When we are able to accurately describe or model the behavior, the best way to organize and manage emerge.

The notion that everyone needs to understand and communicate what is or should be going on is a relatively new concept in today's workplace. There will be more details later in the book on the possibility and value of full transparency after the introduction of Work Models as a way to represent the work of the business as a whole, its core processes, jobs or work groups. This recent notion indicates the recognition of the difficulty inherent in organizing and running a company effectively and efficiently unless everyone truly understands their own and others' work.

The work of an enterprise can be viewed as a systemic relationship between and among certain behavior elements that can then be manipulated to the best ends of the business. This is roughly analogous to knowing the notes of a song so that all the musicians can sing or play individual parts and even develop new music. Using the same knowledge, everyone can then understand what the work is supposed to be and, if it isn't, the right ways to improve the enterprise. There is no one better to make these suggestions and changes than those who do the work, and that is equally true for organizing the enterprise.

For our purposes in this book, everyone can engage in the organization of work—not just management. Management can find the best ways to meet their business circumstances and needs as an enterprise, but the workforce can tell us how to organize their work to achieve those ends.

There are six interrelated elements that together comprise work behavior and can be used to define, align, and organize work. The six elements—the Work Formula—are presented here in two categories based on a cause-and-effect behavioral relationship. In this way, we will see what to produce (the effect) and how to achieve it (the cause).

We begin with the effect of the Work Formula, because in analyzing the work of a business, we must first know the intended results of the work and only then look at how these results are achieved. Thus, our behavioral relationship here is effect and cause. This is consistent with any good business practice. It says we need to know where we are going before determining how to get there.

1—DESIRED EFFECT
Something brought about by a cause or agent; a result

Business *effect* is composed of two interrelated behavior elements: *outputs* and desired *consequences*.

Outputs and Consequences

In work we want to achieve, as an effect, certain deliverables, behaviorally known as outputs, that will result in desired consequences (or benefits or value added). The outputs the business desires are commonly known as products and/or services. We produce or deliver these for the desired positive consequences such as profit, client satisfaction, return on investment, societal good, etc.

If we begin by defining our desired outputs—what products and/or services we want to deliver—and what desired consequences these will need to achieve, we establish the kind of business ends we want to have. We could, conversely, first define what desired consequences we want to achieve, and then what outputs would help us meet those consequences. As a matter of practicality, which of these two elements is defined first or second is often an iterative activity designed to achieve as much clarity of intended business ends or *effect* as possible.

One business desires to produce hamburgers, while another has laptop computers as outputs, and both desire certain consequences like profits, customer satisfaction, return on investment, and so on. In this method of organizing a business, we will therefore begin the definition of work at each level (business unit, core processes, jobs and work groups) by defining and aligning outputs and consequences commensurate with that level of work and in relation to any previous levels already defined (e.g., how jobs relate to the core processes).

The question to be answered in defining or redefining the business after the desired effects have first been delineated is: What does it take, from a purely work perspective, to produce the products/services—the outputs—and the consequences?

2—CAUSE
The producer of an effect or result

Business *cause* is composed of four interrelated behavioral elements: *inputs, conditions, process steps,* and *feedback.*

Interrelated work elements that produce effects (outputs and consequences) include inputs, conditions, process steps, and feedback. Together these four elements are the causes in a cause-and-effect relationship. Each of the four elements has a further systemic relationship to one another that produces the desired effects. Operationally, work can be illustrated as follows:

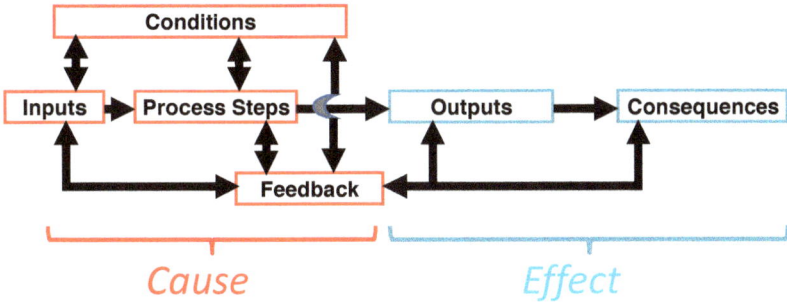

Figure 3

The systemic relationship among these six elements of work can be summarized in the following way:

> *Initiated by and using inputs (such as client need and available resources), under the influence of given or implied conditions (rules and regulations), process steps are followed to produce/provide desired outputs and their associated positive consequences, with the aid of a variety of feedback.*

Note: In our various books and articles on the Language of Work, we have used a variety of terminology to designate work, such as: "deliverables" for outputs, "governances" for conditions, and "work support" for organizational support. Either set of words works well in any business setting and may be mixed and matched as they best communicate meaning and use in your particular setting.

In light of what we have learned thus far in this book, it would be accurate to also add that:

Work is best accomplished when the enterprise provides adequate organizational support to accomplish work execution.

As depicted in the above illustration, the Language of Work is based on a behavioral model, not dissimilar to descriptions of everyday individual behavior. For example, buying food at the grocery store would be a typical output for the consequence of feeding yourself and your family. You bring with you a list of things to buy—your inputs. You have conditions to follow, such as where the food is located in the store, perhaps your dietary needs, coupons, etc. Your process is to traverse the aisles until you find items, put them in your basket and check out. You utilize or seek feedback in various forms of communication as you ask a clerk where to find the cottage cheese, read posted prices, use your smartphone, see whether a particular coupon is useful or not, or communicate with your spouse for those items you may have forgotten.

The six elements of work can similarly be used to explain what work is, or should be, in an enterprise at different levels. By using such a work formula with management and the workforce, we can define and agree on what the business is (its *as-is state*) or should be (its *to-be state*). The work formula can be an invaluable tool in making changes to the enterprise. We will now provide a brief overview as an introduction to the six elements that will comprise what will become a formula for work.

Inputs

One kind of input is familiar and obvious to most of us: the resources used or needed to do the work. However, another kind of input may not seem so obvious, but is always present, necessary and critical to business success. That is the input which initiates or triggers the work. Thus, when a customer says, "I want this," that is the trigger to start work. Similarly when a customer, an executive, manager, or other worker asks for something, it triggers work in the form of the answer to a question, a requested report, a specific task or set of tasks, and so forth.

Conditions (Governances)

Conditions are the rules and regulations that must be taken into account in the execution of work at all levels of work. These conditions are kinds of "inputs" in one sense, but the difference between conditions and inputs is that the conditions are usually "fixed" (much like a rule or policy) and in place. Conditions may be hard to change, but it is not always impossible to do so. Generally speaking individuals can't or really shouldn't change conditions on their own. In business you can ignore conditions, but that really isn't that smart. Instead, you can learn what to do with them and influence how they might be used or changed.

Conditions are of two types: internal and external. Internal conditions are typically found in company policy and procedures manuals. Various external governing sources would include such things as laws, regulations, union rules, and so forth. Following OSHA rules on safety would be a good example. Conditions commonly have influence over inputs used, process steps to be followed, and even feedback.

In the grocery shopping illustration cited above, typical conditions would include store layout, nutritional listings, return policies, use of coupons, etc.

Process Steps

Process steps, or procedures, are the activity engaged in to produce the outputs of work. When an input, such as a client request, presents itself, we initiate a series of actions to respond to or service the request. It may be a process that requires a repetitious set of steps or one or more sets of steps that allow workers to "create" the way the request will be accomplished. Process steps are what we commonly think of as the activity, the tasks, of doing work.

Feedback

Feedback includes the information that helps us do the work correctly, helps make us take corrective actions, reinforces us when we have done things right or shows us when we've done them wrong.

There are two broad forms of feedback. The first we use while working and the other occurs when the work is finished. Thus there is "during feedback," or more technically a *formative* kind of feedback from managers, other workers, and clients that help get the work done correctly and on time; here we can make any needed mid-course corrections. Then, there is "after feedback," or a *summative* kind that says we have done the work right, and the customer is satisfied (e.g., repeatedly purchasing our output). Or, conversely, the work output isn't exactly what they wanted and needs to be corrected in some way. Note that feedback is systemically related to the other five elements of work, as illustrated here:

Input: we correctly heard the customer's request

Process Steps: we completed the procedure the right way, or we have seen it needs to be adjusted

Conditions: we followed the rules or regulations

Outputs: we gave the customer the right product or service, as requested

Consequences: the customer says he or she is satisfied and pays us

Feedback is perhaps the most overlooked element of work in business.

Examples of each of the six elements of the Language of Work for the grocery purchasing example are summarized in Figure 4. Note carefully how each element has a systemic cause-and-effect relationship to others.

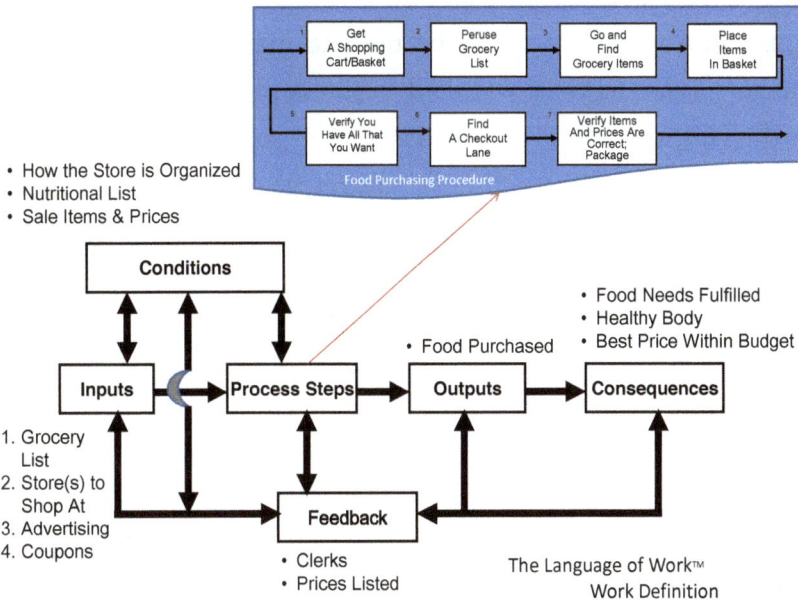

Figure 4

This Work Formula, as we will come to refer to it, serves as the anchor for defining work behaviorally. With this in mind, we can now look at how it would be used to organize an enterprise. In broad terms, this means we need to define and reach consensus on the four levels of work, as well as on how to support the work as an enterprise by using the Work Formula. This defining process—or modeling, as you will come to know it—will lead to a deep knowledge of the business and tell you how best to structure it.

With a Work Formula to define and agree on, it is now possible to achieve work alignment of a different kind than ever before. This is the alignment of the business WHAT, HOW, WHO, and WORK GROUPS, as well as linking them to WORK STANDARDS, WORK SUPPORT, HUMAN RELATIONS, and FINANCIAL SUPPORT.

Not only does the Work Formula help achieve work alignment, but as you will learn it can be used to manage the work, all of this in service to your well-laid business plans, strategies, and so forth. This kind of alignment cannot be solely attained by good intentions or even by well-defined strategies, plans, and processes. No matter how well we construct and understand business plans, they almost always lack an operational view of how the work will be accomplished. Such an operational view is made possible and embedded in the Work Formula of the Language of Work.

Figure 5 illustrates how using the Language of Work™ to define work at the four levels and layers of work allows—indeed, demands—alignment among the levels and layers of work. Because the Language of Work is both systemic and systematic, its use allows work to be defined by the same six elements of work. Using these six elements to define work at the various levels and layers inside complex organizations provides universal clarity to all areas of work and among everyone in the organization.

**The Alignment of Work Execution and Work Support
Using the Language of Work™**

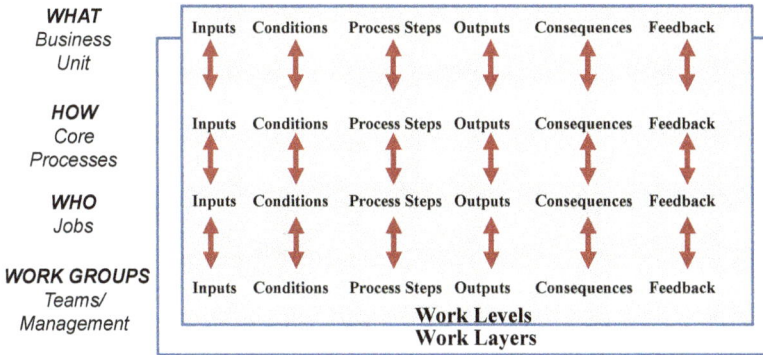

	Inputs	Conditions	Process Steps	Outputs	Consequences	Feedback
WHAT *Business Unit*						
HOW *Core Processes*	Inputs	Conditions	Process Steps	Outputs	Consequences	Feedback
WHO *Jobs*	Inputs	Conditions	Process Steps	Outputs	Consequences	Feedback
WORK GROUPS *Teams/ Management*	Inputs	Conditions	Process Steps	Outputs	Consequences	Feedback

Work Levels
Work Layers

© 2000 Performance International
Based on The Language of Work Model™

Figure 5

As such, it also provides a degree of transparency never realized before. We shall now see how this plays out through a sample Business Model using the 6-4-4 paradigm of the Language of Work that you can replicate in your own business.

Chapter 6

Work Analytics for the Business Model

The authors have devised a set of ways (tools) to actualize the Work Formula for defining and implementing the Business Model, *The Managing Model*, and *The Working Model* (the subjects of other books in *The Work Trilogy*).

These Work Analytic Tools (WATs), as we refer to them, make applying the work formula easy and useful for

> This chapter introduces a set of analytical tools that can be used to develop, implement, and continuously improve the Business Model

defining, implementing, and measuring work to meet business needs. These tools include such things as work models, matrices, the Work Formula itself, and other tools that will be introduced in this and the other two books of *The Work Trilogy*. Relative to the Business Model, we introduce two Work Analytic Tools known as work models and work matrices.

Work Models

There are four basic kinds of work models; each one reflecting a different work execution level:

> Business Unit Model
> Core Processes Models
> Job Models
> Work Group Models

As generically illustrated in Figures 6 and 7, Work models are a specialized LoW version of flowcharting incorporating all six elements of the Work Formula. Not only do the work models help portray what work is to be achieved and how at each level, but they also show the relationship—alignment—to each other. This alignment helps ensure overall work efficiency and effectiveness.

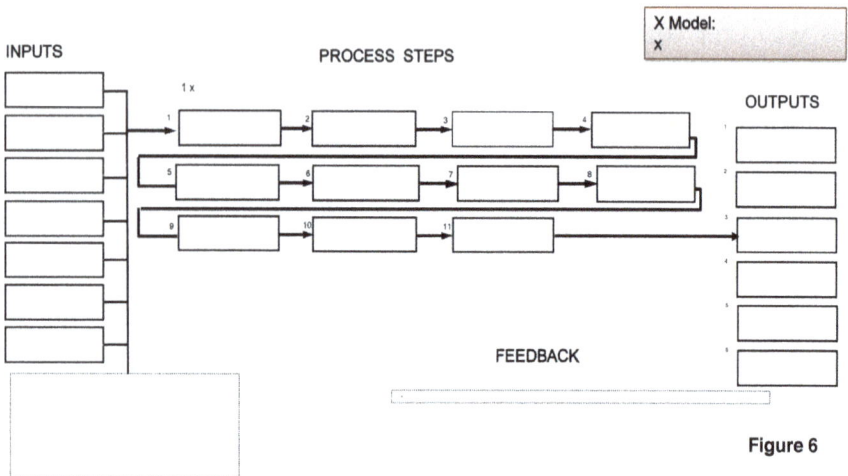

Figure 6

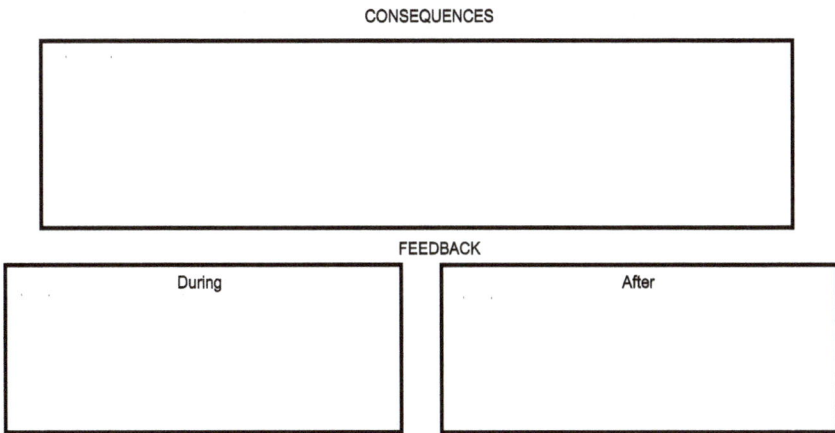

CONSEQUENCES

FEEDBACK

During	After

Figure 7

Models may be represented in a state of TO BE, a state of AS IS, or both, as needed. If desired, they may also be used to achieve a level of work transparency never before realized.

Work Matrices

Work matrices are used to display the layers of work that an organization must assure are in place to maintain work execution. These matrices relate to work standards, work support, human relations, and financial support. Each matrix employs the work formula on one axis within the context of the four levels of work execution. As you will learn and see later, each point of congruence in the matrix is populated with measurement data, programs, performance indicators, and services that are needed or measured in an organization to maintain and support work execution. These matrices may be used both to decide what work layer support is desired, and to help in the continuous evaluation of their merit on an ongoing basis, helping to determine what work support needs improving. We recommend that you tailor the matrices to your specific business environment. Figure 8 illustrates a sample work matrix—in this case for work support without the data in each box.

WORK SUPPORT MATRIX

	INPUT	CONDITIONS	PROCESS	OUTPUT	CONSEQUENCES	FEEDBACK
BUSINESS UNIT	STRATEGY & BUS. PLANS	CULTURE / CONTROLS	ADMINISTRATIVE SYSTEMS	BUSINESS DELIVERABLES	BUSINESS RESULTS	BUSINESS MEASUREM./EVALUAT.
	1A	1B	1C	1D	1E	1F
CORE PROCESSES	PROCESS RESOURCES	REGULATIONS/ POLICIES	TECHNOLOGIES (SOFT & HARD)	PROCESS DELIVERABLES	PROCESS RESULTS	CONFIRMATIONS & CORRECTIONS
	2A	2B	2C	2D	2E	2F
JOBS	CLIENT NEEDS & RESOURCES	WORK INFLUENCES	WORK METHODS	JOB DELIVERABLES	INDIVIDUAL RESULTS	CONFIRMATIONS & SELF ADJUSTMENT
	3A	3B	3C	3D	3E	3F
WORK GROUPS	CLIENT NEEDS & RESOURCES	VALUES & PRACTICES	INTERFACE/ RELATIONSHIPS	WORK GROUP DELIVERABLES	WORK GROUP RESULTS	MANAGEMENT/TEAM INFORMATION SYSTEM
	4A	4B	4C	4D	4E	4F

Figure 8

Both forms of WATs will be illustrated in the business modeling example that follows.

In addition, throughout *The Work Trilogy* you will find a range of other Work Analytic Tools that are used to operationalize the Work Formula for executives, managers, and workers including the following:

- As Is/To Be Tables and Models
- Dots On Models
- Work Plan
- Jobs Identified to Processes

- Work Analysis Aid
- Cultural Audit
- Worker Verbatim
- Etc.

Chapter 7

A Sample LoW Business Model: (Part 1)

This introductory example of a Business Model based on the Language of Work occurred in a major utility with a large IT function. We will call it Agua IT Services (AITS), a fictional name to preserve confidentiality. AITS has about 250 employees; its mission is to provide several services related to statewide

> This chapter introduces a case study of an actual Business Model. The emphasis is on the four levels of work execution.

water management, flood control, environmental concerns, agricultural and citizenry needs related to the transport and the availability of water statewide. The IT business unit services more than 50 internal business units and provides a wide range of IT services for monitoring, conveying, protecting, and maintaining the quality of water resources. AITS largely employs IT professionals, technicians, specialists, and support personnel.

First, Define the Business Unit: The "WHAT"

To achieve organizational alignment (as well as transparency and continuous improvement), an enterprise must begin with a clear understanding (especially among executives) of WHAT the enterprise is (its current state) or is to be (its future state). This should be obvious enough, since we all agree that knowing the goal is critical to achieving that goal. However, as stated in Chapter 2, companies often grow in bits and pieces, or in spurts, which then leads to an absence of deep, universal understanding of the work. An operational model—such as the Language of Work—to define the "what" and reach consensus overcomes deficiencies in work understanding. For this reason, with rare exceptions, we must begin the organization at the business unit level.

The AITS executive team formed for organizing the IT business began defining their business unit by identifying major outputs as listed in Figure 9. These are the major products and services that they "deliver" to their customers (mainly water contractors) and clients (internal business units, agricultural groups, and citizens). These are primarily services like IT Flood Management, Telecom Services, SAP Installation and Administration, Data Software Support, Project Management, and so forth. Most enterprises deliver 5 to 7 major outputs, but there are exceptions. In the case of AITS, there were 10 major outputs, a few of which are listed in Figure 9.

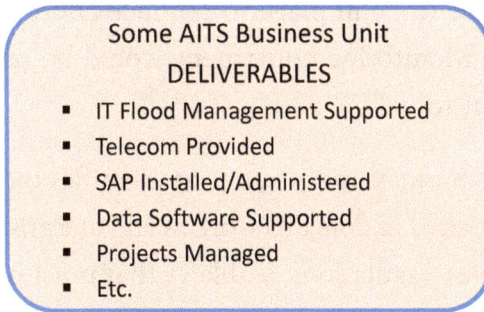

Figure 9

Note on the chart: We are deliberately not listing all outputs produced by AITS; instead, we are providing a few examples so that you can see the work-product without getting caught up in the details of a typical work model. If you want more detail, this may be found in other sources, such as the many organization engagement case studies available from the authors.

For AITS to achieve its desired outputs (and consequences) they need the means to do so. In the Language of Work, those "means" are the four work elements: inputs, conditions, process steps, and feedback.

Looking at inputs first, remember that inputs are of two kinds: triggers and resources. We see that AITS inputs include various kinds of client requests that trigger work, as well as a variety of resources which are needed to accomplish the processes, adhere to the conditions and utilize the feedback. *Trigger inputs* articulate the initiators of the work; this is important because when these inputs are enhanced or improved, they directly impact the quality and/or amount of output. The more client requests there are, such as, in this case, from *water contractors*, the greater the quantity of (work) output should result. The other kinds of inputs, known as *resources*, identify what needs to be in place to produce and/or service the business outputs. Monitoring equipment would be one example of a resource input for AITS.

The enterprise business unit team next identifies the conditions that need to be satisfied in doing its work as an enterprise. These are most often the rules, regulations, and laws that must be followed. These are, so to speak, the "stay out of jail" elements of work. Federal regulations govern water resource utilization stringently in the case of AITS. Other examples (in red) of inputs and conditions to the business unit model of AITS are listed in Figure 10:

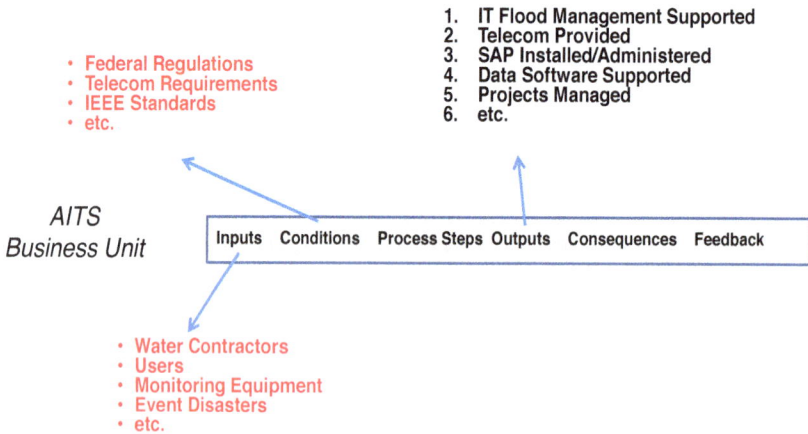

Figure 10

After the outputs, inputs, and conditions are defined, the business unit modeling team turns its attention to the desired consequences for AITS, answering the question, "What are the outputs designed to be achieved as value-add?" Usually the consequences are pretty straightforward, and executives have little difficulty identifying them. The consequences are expressed as value statements of desired business outcomes that include things like: reliable IT systems, 24-7 IT coverage, protection of employee and public confidentiality, satisfaction of end-to-end client needs, and so on. One of the ways to ensure that the desired consequences have all been identified is to cross-reference the consequences with the outputs that should achieve them.

Note: This model is designed in such a way that, by using techniques such as cross- referencing outputs with consequences, one is assured that all the outputs have been named.

For those wondering why consequence is defined fourth, rather than first or in conjunction with outputs, it is simply that our experience in modeling hundreds of work models demonstrates that there is a best practice in the order of defining the six work elements. This principally arises out of the value of knowing inputs and conditions prior to defining consequences, since both have a strong influence on the nature and scope of consequences. The authors recognize there are circumstances in which beginning with consequences, then determining what outputs produce these consequences (e.g., when defining a new business) is suggested. You may try either way, understanding that in the final analysis modeling is a very iterative process in which all elements are clarified as additional, subsequent definition of all work elements is undertaken.

Any missing consequences, or for that matter incomplete outputs, will be revealed by cross-checking; missing refinements will emerge in the subsequent definition of process steps and other work elements. For the AITS business unit, some outputs and consequences are summarized below, to which examples of the other work elements will be added shortly.

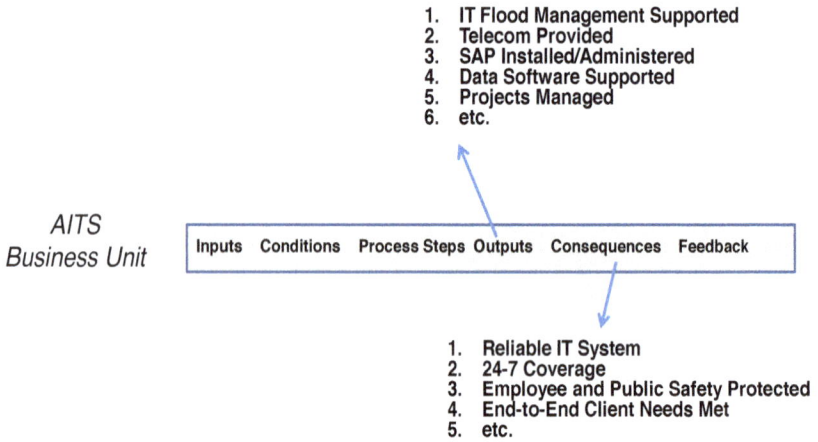

1. **IT Flood Management Supported**
2. **Telecom Provided**
3. **SAP Installed/Administered**
4. **Data Software Supported**
5. **Projects Managed**
6. **etc.**

AITS
Business Unit

Inputs	Conditions	Process Steps	Outputs	Consequences	Feedback

1. **Reliable IT System**
2. **24-7 Coverage**
3. **Employee and Public Safety Protected**
4. **End-to-End Client Needs Met**
5. **etc.**

Figure 11

Once the outputs, inputs, conditions, and consequences have been identified, the team modeling the business unit is in a position to model the process steps at the business unit level relative to each output, given that the inputs, under the conditions, will produce the outputs that achieve the consequences.

The business unit category "process steps" is most often an organizational depiction of work groups. The business unit's process steps will therefore be defined in a form different from the process steps of the other three levels of work execution. This is because the detail needed to achieve consensus on process steps at the business unit level is far less. Additionally, executives, for their part, are mostly interested in a high-level view of the business unit process steps. They don't need or desire details on work execution that others, like managers and workers, need. When and if they should eventually need work details, these are available through other core process, job, and/or work group models.

An illustration from the AITS business unit will adequately illustrate one—a primary, but not exclusive—version for expressing process steps in a business unit.

The process steps of the AITS As Is Business Unit shown in Figure 12 illustrate how work is processed organizationally. This is fairly typical of how enterprises represent themselves. The org. chart illustrates the relationship of various work groups (departments, entities, etc.). It communicates how AITS views, from a process steps point of view, the achievement of its major outputs and consequences.

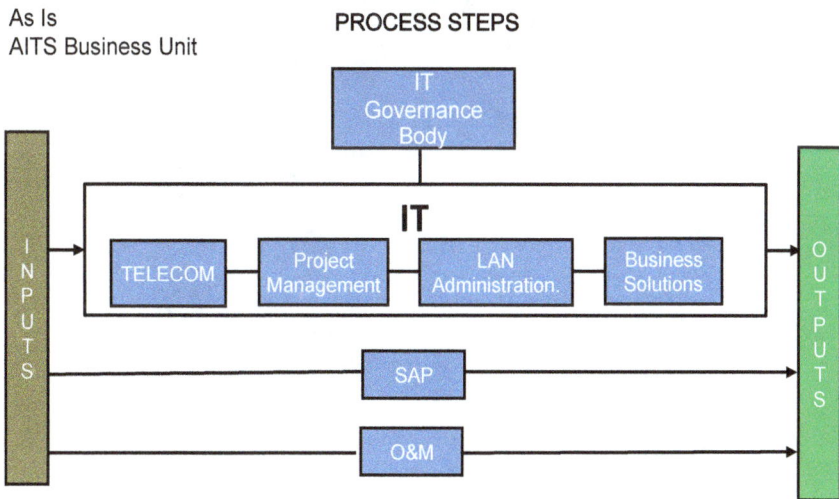

Figure 12

This stage of depicting a business unit process steps is merely a first draft placeholder. It shows the current, AS IS, state of the process steps AITS uses as a business unit. In the future state of modeling the business unit (the TO BE state), the new organization structure that results after alignment of work from business unit to core processes to jobs and finally to work groups will emerge. Thus, the TO BE process of the business unit will emerge nearly at the end of the entire modeling process. Only then can we be assured that the best organization for the enterprise is based on an alignment of the work, defined throughout the organization from one level to the next, which culminates in determination of work groups.

There are several ways to formulate process steps of a business unit according to varying business needs and desires. These ways are summarized in Figure 13.

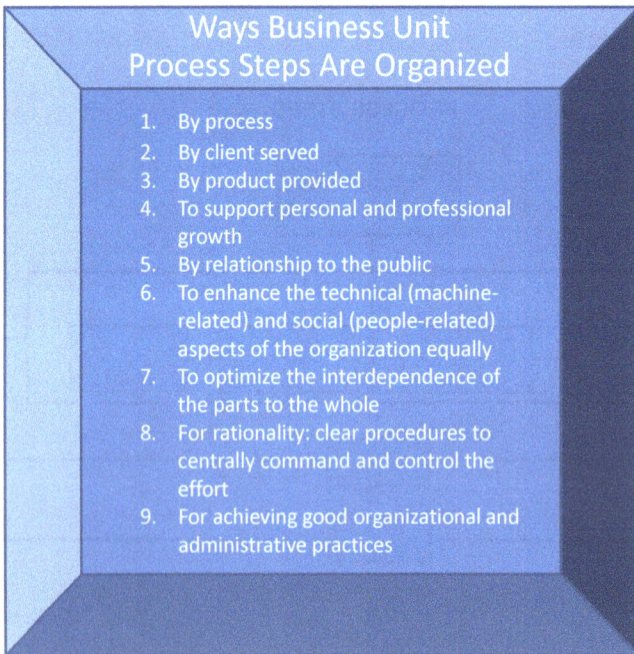

Ways Business Unit Process Steps Are Organized

1. By process
2. By client served
3. By product provided
4. To support personal and professional growth
5. By relationship to the public
6. To enhance the technical (machine-related) and social (people-related) aspects of the organization equally
7. To optimize the interdependence of the parts to the whole
8. For rationality: clear procedures to centrally command and control the effort
9. For achieving good organizational and administrative practices

Figure 13

Among these, the easiest and most often used is number 8, a perceived need for "clear procedures to centrally command and control the effort." This is reflected in the process steps in the AITS enterprise: It illustrates how all the various work groups relate to one another to produce the outputs, using a hierarchical/military central command structure.

Still another way to represent process steps in a business unit is by the flow of different core processes—criterion one in the table of how business units are commonly organized. Thus, for example, the process of marketing flows into the processes of selling, delivering, billing, and customer servicing. This would be an example of the business unit process steps in other enterprises. Regardless of which criterion you chose, the business unit modeling need at this point is to capture at a high-level view of how work flows to achieve the **outputs** and **consequences** by using the **inputs**, adhering to **conditions**, and aided by appropriate **feedback**. There is no need at this stage of modeling the business unit for lots of core process detail for each business deliverable.

Finally, we come to defining feedback as the sixth work element of a business unit model. At the business unit level, feedback is key to knowing that the organization is doing its work right and can make mid-course corrections when needed. Ultimately feedback ensures that the clients and customers receiving the outputs are satisfied. Figure 14 lists some typical examples of business-unit-level feedback for the AITS enterprise.

Thus, by way of summary, the six elements of work are used to define and achieve an understanding and consensus of AITS at the business unit level. Business unit modeling by the executives achieves agreement on the WHAT of the business. This model sets the direction for communicating to everyone in the modeling process exactly what the executives want the work of

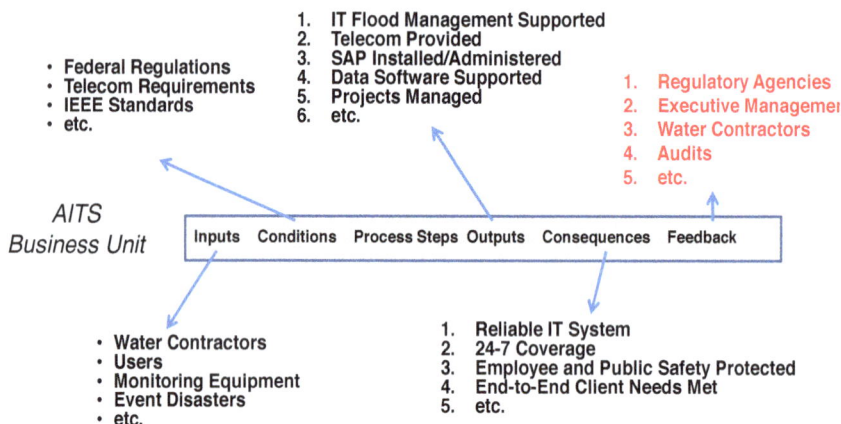

Figure 14

the enterprise to be. Others in the enterprise will then base their modeling of core processes, jobs, work groups/management, and various layers of needed support on this graphic understanding/modeling of the business unit.

Second, Define and Align Core Processes to the Business Unit: The "HOW" with the "WHAT"

With the business unit well-defined and shared with others for input, clarification, and consensus, the modeling of the business moves next to the core processes. These are needed to make clear how the business specifically intends to produce the products and services (outputs). Now is when much of the detail—but still only at a level that adequately communicates—begins to emerge as to how the work is to be done to achieve those major outputs. This is done—and this is important—without general regard for WHO will actually do the work. As noted previously, in the Language of Work approach WHO comes at the third level of work modeling—the job level. WHO (individually) is obviously important, but to achieve alignment, the organization must first define the optimal view of how the work is to be done. Otherwise the core process can be derailed into discussions of a lack of perceived talent or concerns about taking care of or finding a place for individuals. Be prepared to define core processes ideally, but realistically, given available technology and resources. Thinking outside the box when defining core processes can pay immense dividends to making work and the organization all that much better.

We will look at the core process of AITS related to the output of *SAP installed and administered*, and within that core process, *reports produced*. Therefore, the corollary process name is *producing reports*.

Core processes are best modeled by management at the operational level; usually by directors, managers, and/or supervisory personnel—those whom everyone in the enterprise generally acknowledge for their expertise at the core process level. They usually have the respect of both the executive management and the workforce. It is desirable for an exemplary job performer in a given core process to be on the core process modeling team. Their perspective adds much value and often keeps management personnel more realistic.

As we have noted, core processes represent the HOW of the business. They show how to produce the major outputs that have been specified in the business unit model. Since the Work Formula is used to define both business unit and core processes, the six elements of work in both can be precisely aligned with one another: outputs of business unit to outputs of core processes, inputs of business unit to inputs to core processes, and so forth for the other four elements of work. Of course, they will be defined at differing levels of detail, but they can and should be aligned. Not aligning the work in this way only places workgroups at odds with one another and creates great inefficiency or even conflict among workers and managers.

As was noted before, the modeling of core processes is done by key managers and exemplary performers, under sponsorship and with involvement by executives. They define each model, preferably with a good facilitator. Your managers will be producing, in this phase of the work modeling process, a clear, concise, and consensus-based view of HOW this work will be done to align with the executive view of WHAT the business is. Once everyone understands the alignment of the HOW with the WHAT, modeling can move to the next step: WHO will do the work to achieve that HOW. Part of the AITS core process for *producing reports* is illustrated in Figure 15:

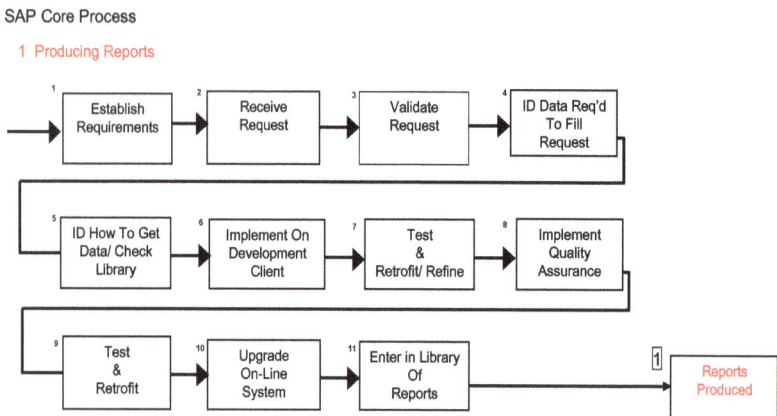

SAP Core Process

1 Producing Reports

1 Establish Requirements	2 Receive Request	3 Validate Request	4 ID Data Req'd To Fill Request

5 ID How To Get Data/ Check Library	6 Implement On Development Client	7 Test & Retrofit/ Refine	8 Implement Quality Assurance

9 Test & Retrofit	10 Upgrade On-Line System	11 Enter in Library Of Reports	1 Reports Produced

Figure 15

Third, Define Jobs by Aligning to the Core Processes using the Work Formula: The "WHO" to the "HOW"

Alignment of Work Levels

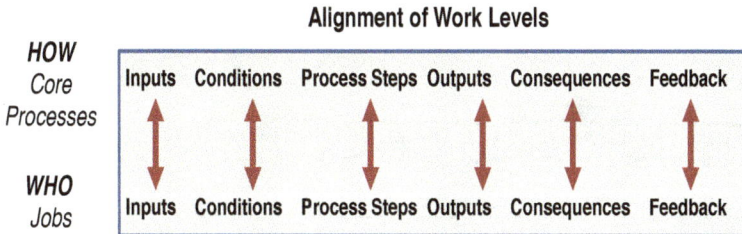

Figure 16

There is a maxim that goes: "Success depends on matching the right person to the right job!" A precursor of this maxim should be: "To get the right job, match all jobs to their related core processes." It's not enough to select the right person to implement a job role; it must be the right job for the work itself. This mismatch happens more often than you may think. But now there is a much more scientific way to place people in jobs than turning over a list of specifications (dream team or job characteristics, perhaps) to HR. Instead, by aligning jobs to the core processes, you can be sure that you are defining the *right* jobs to fill.

The Language of Work solves the identification of jobs quite simply. Once core processes have been modeled (as described in the second step above), one can simply list the job titles that currently exist (and/or new job roles that are revealed from core process modeling), and color code these jobs to the process steps of the core processes. Figure 17 is a simplified illustration of how this looks relative to the sample SAP core process and the output that relates to *producing reports*:

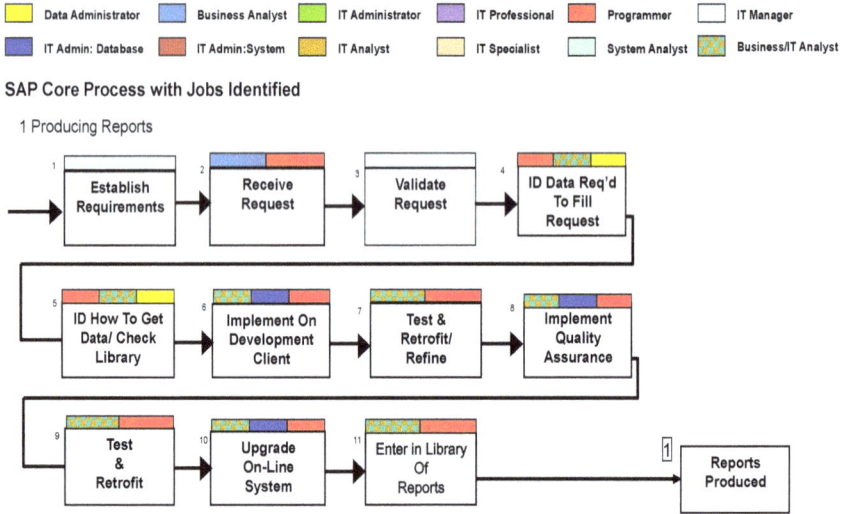

Figure 17

When jobs are modeled using the Work Formula approach, existing job holders will not be left to decide for themselves (or told by managers or HR), what their jobs entail. Instead, each job will begin with the understanding of how that job fits into the core processes of the business. Because jobs are based operationally on the work needed to execute the well-defined and aligned core processes, through color-coding jobs to the core processes, each job can subsequently be modeled based on the actual work to be performed. Use the Work Formula to model these jobs, with primary input coming from the core process models. Ordinary job descriptions cannot do this, because the relation of the job to the core process has not been linked. The succeeding alignment process inherent in the Business Model will help ensure that you have the right jobs for your core processes; then, and only then, will you be able to find the right person(s) to do the work consistently and well.

The six elements of the Work Formula can be used to define any job, no matter how simple or complex the work. Job models precisely connected to the six elements of work previously defined in the core processes and business unit are critical to a well-designed, well-aligned enterprise.

Fourth, Model and Align the Work Groups/Management: Work Groups Aligned to Jobs, Core Processes and the Business Unit

Individual job holders don't typically work in a vacuum. Rather, they work with other professionals, technicians, and support staff, and with managers who help facilitate the work. Individual jobs need to be aligned with other related jobs in the enterprise. We refer to the jobs that relate to one another as the Work Group/Management level of work execution; business also refers to this level by names like teams, units, sections, or departments. These are all one version or another of what we collectively label as *work groups*. One of the greatest features of the Language of Work is that it provides the means to align work groups and management positions directly to the

> The organizational structure, by virtue of using the Language of Work approach, practically reveals itself from the preceding modeling that has taken place through the various work levels.

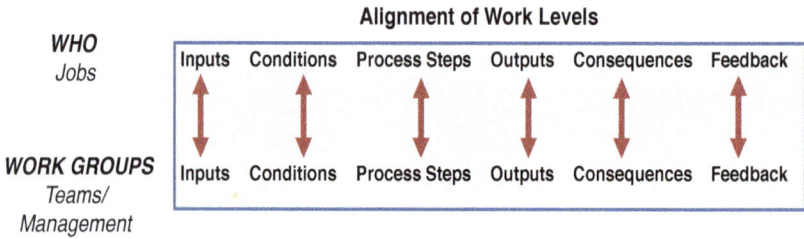

Alignment of Work Levels

	Inputs	Conditions	Process Steps	Outputs	Consequences	Feedback
WHO *Jobs*						
WORK GROUPS *Teams/ Management*	Inputs	Conditions	Process Steps	Outputs	Consequences	Feedback

Figure 18

business unit, core processes and jobs, as shown in Figure 18. This creates unity in the work and eliminates disconnects.

Teams are generally decided based on the flow of *core processes*, but not exclusively. Thus, a team may be organized to complete a whole core process, across core processes, or as a part of a core process. Then again, other factors may come to play in deciding what the teams need to be, such as those listed in Figure 19:

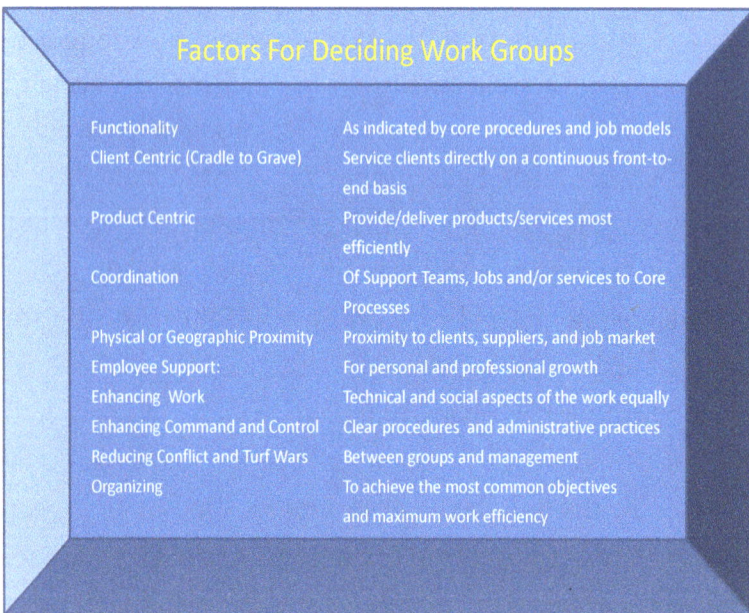

Factors For Deciding Work Groups

Functionality	As indicated by core procedures and job models
Client Centric (Cradle to Grave)	Service clients directly on a continuous front-to-end basis
Product Centric	Provide/deliver products/services most efficiently
Coordination	Of Support Teams, Jobs and/or services to Core Processes
Physical or Geographic Proximity	Proximity to clients, suppliers, and job market
Employee Support:	For personal and professional growth
Enhancing Work	Technical and social aspects of the work equally
Enhancing Command and Control	Clear procedures and administrative practices
Reducing Conflict and Turf Wars	Between groups and management
Organizing	To achieve the most common objectives and maximum work efficiency

Figure 19

In AITS, IT professionals were placed in work groups based on their functionality in producing common outputs—for example, *IT support services* or *SAP support*. Jobs in these work groups interacted with other work groups like *engineering science services & support,* or *end-user support*. Each of these work groups is modeled using the same six-element Work Formula of the Language of Work. This allows the various jobs, core processes, and the business unit models to be aligned with one another.

As is true of other work execution levels, the modeling of work groups is best done by a facilitator with exemplary job performers who are or will be part of the work group. They follow the order of modeling of the six work elements, as was previously done with the business unit, core processes, and jobs. Thus, each modeling output becomes the input to the next level of work execution organization.

Once identified and modeled, the work groups will collectively form the basis of the second part of organization—what is commonly thought of as the organizational structure. This also becomes the TO BE (future) process step of the business unit model, substituting in the Business Model for what was, before the use of the LoW, modeled as an organizational chart. An Org Chart can be retained or modified, but it is not really a tool for work alignment; rather, it is a communication tool of management hierarchy.

You will find that the organizational structure, by virtue of using the Language of Work approach, practically reveals itself from the modeling that has taken place through the various work levels. This is because there is a kind of cumulative intelligence that the various preceding modeling reveals about how to organize the work groups. Such "organization intel," as we might label it, is hard to describe without direct experience of the use of the Business Model approach, but it invariably will clearly reveal what the organization chart—or, more accurately, the process step of the business unit—should be. Additionally, some other organization intel is garnered by reviewing best practices on the internet and through other professional resources.

Thus, AITS discovered through the various modeling processes that some of its major outputs were best accomplished on a decentralized basis. In so doing, they could service the organization-wide needs of the whole enterprise much more efficiently, saving substantially on costs, while allowing highly specialized IT services to be performed by technical people with other job duties.

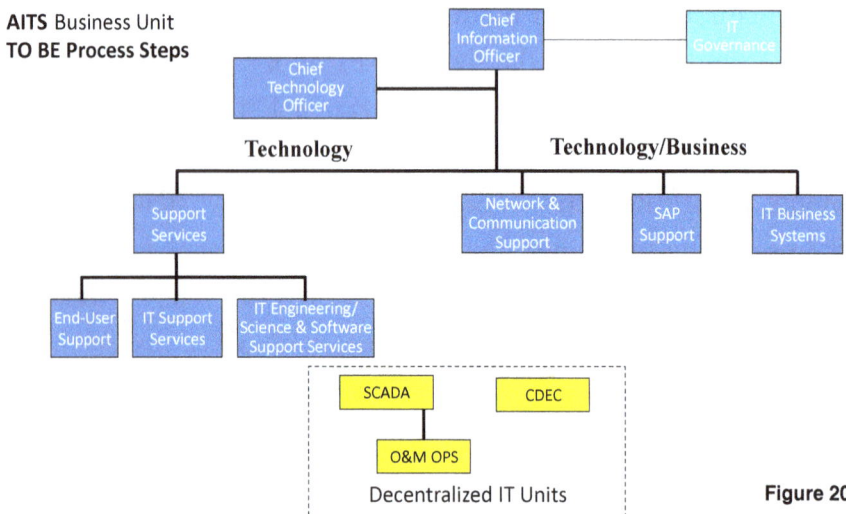

AITS Business Unit
TO BE Process Steps

Chief Information Officer

IT Governance

Chief Technology Officer

Technology

Technology/Business

Support Services

Network & Communication Support

SAP Support

IT Business Systems

End-User Support

IT Support Services

IT Engineering/ Science & Software Support Services

SCADA

CDEC

O&M OPS

Decentralized IT Units

Figure 20

Just a few notes about this structure:

1. The Language of Work made it clear that some needed work was not being done. Specifically, the business of IT—that is, investigating new technologies and new needs, planning, budgeting, and coordinating efforts—was not being performed in an organized fashion. The new structure created a unit that approached IT from a business perspective. This decentralized group also served as a project management office so that new initiatives could be managed centrally after approval. In addition, it was clear that an expert in emerging technologies possessed a different skillset from a good administrator of a current IT unit. The new structure therefore demonstrated the need for a Chief Technology Officer whose job included ensuring that AITS was prepared to adopt new technologies as they became generally available.

2. Another need the models revealed was that of providing consulting services to various scientific and engineering offices within the business. Before the Language of Work, the centralized IT function provided little support to line departments. They therefore had created a mini-IT unit themselves, or were accustomed to using very expensive talent (usually PhDs in scientific areas) to replace, order, and install new software and hardware or repair broken servers. In the new structure, scientists only serviced science-based technology. Technology common to all was serviced by the newly structured, centralized IT department.

3. You see three decentralized IT units above on the chart of the business unit future process steps. Because these three units had technology that was different from that of most other units in the enterprise, it was determined that they would keep a small IT function within their own departments. The rationale was that the centralized IT department would serve units which had similar needs across the organization. Decentralized units would service others only when there was unit-specific technology in those units.

Once the new (TO BE) business unit process step has been identified, the third step of organization related to work groups is then to identify the various management role needs, although some become apparent as the alignment of work unfolds. As with all the operational, technical and support jobs already modeled in the Business Model, management jobs are then modeled using the same six-element Work Formula.

These management jobs are for work groups or across work groups that clearly need to be managed, and the model shows how. A manager's job will be defined to reflect how he or she should facilitate individuals and the team, as well as their interaction, as needed, with other work groups. Management job models provide a very clear way of giving meaning to how to coach, schedule, give feedback, review job performance, and the like. They also provide insights into how to ensure that inputs provided by other units are timely and well used—especially how to manage what has become known as the "white space." These and many other aspects of facilitating work are further identified and explained in *The Managing Model* of *The Work Trilogy*. Executives will see clearly how managers manage work more effectively and in alignment with the different levels of the enterprise.

In summary, from the overall description and illustration of the sample Business Model in this chapter, it should now be possible to see that the Language of Work is a highly systematic process. It organizes by modeling and aligning succeeding work execution levels. It remains only now to learn how to align work standards, work support, human relations, and financial needs to the four levels of work.

This should clearly demonstrate that work at various levels and supported at various layers can be successfully aligned, then constantly reviewed in terms of the systemic relationship that levels and layers have upon one another. Work should not be confusing, inefficient, unclear, or unrelated to common ends. It should, instead, provide optimal service to clients.

To succeed, a business cannot have various groups at odds with one another. There needs to be an alignment and form of transparency that is clearly understood and constantly improved.

Note: If you wish to see the complete AITS Business Unit Model used in this chapter for illustrative purposes, you may access it on our website (www.performanceinternational.com). Look for AQUA Company Case Study in the Books, Case Studies, and Articles pulldown menu. Additional description of the business unit model is found here, as well the sequence for development. You'll also find additional case studies of business modeling that are relevant to your business.

Chapter 8

Aligning the Business Layers to the Levels of Work Execution (Part 2)

Aligning Work Standards

If not mandated or specifically defined as desired, then standards to which work should rise are generally assumed! That is perhaps one of the biggest mistakes an enterprise can make. Expressed in such statements as, "Do it right!" "Do it the way the customer wants it!" Or even, "Do it my way!" and so on, are not exactly useful guides to how well the work should be done, although they certainly are usual. Clearly more useful setting of standards is desirable without overdoing them. Where standards are mandated by law or regulation, one doesn't have much choice other than how these are made known, encouraged, reinforced, and even rewarded. What we will be concerned with in the general application

> Work is more than work execution. What does it take to achieve alignment of work execution with work standards, work support, human relations, and financial support? Without such alignment, work execution cannot reach its maximum potential.

to the Business Model is assuring that standards are set where needed. This will require a systematic approach to deciding what standards are needed for what aspects of work execution.

Standards fall generally into four categories:
- Quantity
- Quality
- Timeliness
- Cost

What aspects of work in an enterprise might need standards? Our focal point for answering this question is quite simple when the Business Model approach is used. Since we utilize a Work Formula to define what the work execution will be, we turn to each of the six elements of work to identify standards when and where needed. A few examples, then introduction of a useful Work Standards Matrix, will assure specification and alignment of standards to work execution.

When you think of the six elements that comprise the formula for work—especially in the cause and effect relationship—we might say the attainment of Consequences is the ultimate goal of standards. We want to achieve maximum customer satisfaction, profit, return on investment, and so forth. Some of these should have numbers and percentages attached to them as standards, while others can be expressed in a more general sense. When it comes to the other five elements of work, however, we may need to be even more explicit and precise. At the same time we don't want to set standards for everything, as doing so becomes meaningless. A systematic approach to deciding standards is suggested.

The following is the LoW Work Standards Matrix.

WORK STANDARDS MATRIX

Inputs	Conditions	Process Steps	Outputs	Consequences	Feedback
QUANTITY Client Needs Identified RFPs responded To Leads Provided Ideas Submitted Documents Available Orders Taken	Litigations Settled Fines Imposed	Breakdowns Steps Hands Touching Revisions Amount of Scrap Milestones Met	Total Sales Total Work Delivered Amount of Service Changes Billable Hours	Work Won ROI Expectations Met Marketshare	Returns QIPs Service Calls Changes
QUALITY All of Client Needs Identified Usability For Processing Servicelife Measure Of Other's Output As My Input	Stability Lemon Laws EEO Guidelines Injuries Compliance	Waste Rejects	Rework Delivery Condition	Recalls Repairs Reject Rate Error-free	Complaints Kinds of QIPs Claims Level of Communication
TIMELINESS Lead Time Just-In-Time Schedule Cycle Time	Conformance Regulation Reports Schedule	Hours Expended Overtime Hours Down-Time Response Time Schedule Cycle Time Delays Due Dates	Delivery Time	Lag Time On-Time	Response Time Schedule Cycle Time
COST Raw Materials Cost Vendor/Supplier Cost	Cost of regulation Budget Variance Budget Hours	Funds Committed Project Cost Labor Cost	Cost/unit	Profitability Cost/Benefits Ratio Value	Sales Figures Cost Per Sale

© 1997 Performance International

Figure 21

This is a sample Work Standards Matrix that we developed for a business that does marketing/sales. It is not a sample matrix that fits all businesses. The Work Standards Matrix needs to be tailored for each business due to their unique business requirements. What is useful is that it is an example of standards identified in the four categories according to the Work Formula. Thus, standards may be specified that would apply and be significant to the business in terms of what it does, how the work is done, who does the work, and for work groups/management. You will find that doing so provides the template for consistently and completely delineating the standards for each different job or other level of work. The determination of such standards can cause a rich discussion among personnel doing and responsible for the work at all levels from executive management to the lowest level of work. Then the standards can be assessed on a continuous basis. We will discuss this at length in the next chapter.

Aligning Work Support

A wise colleague once stated that any good process can be negated in its effectiveness and/or efficiency by a negative work culture. We all know this to be the case. Most of us have worked in companies that are toxic in one form or another and experienced how work suffers as a result. For example, there is the manager who has to have everything done his way. Or the resources that we need to do our job are slow in coming from the outside vendors or from poorly trained individuals internally. Or there is no mechanism for making suggestions. Goals are poorly communicated, and the hierarchy is a "good-old-boys" network. Or a career path is nonexistent. All of these and many other factors have to do with two different layers of work, and we shall distinguish these as being related to either WORK SUPPORT or HUMAN RELATIONS. You can pretty well guess that those factors related to what people do (executives, managers, professionals, and workers) are part of Human Relations, and all other "interventions" belong with Work Support.

We don't want to do careful analyses to model and align work execution and then have it not be effective because the enterprise doesn't provide a healthy work environment. Thus, enterprises need to periodically, if not continuously, conduct cultural due diligence. As a previous analogy noted, due diligence ensures we have healthy water for our swimmers, divers, water polo teams, and the like to swim/work in. Otherwise, continuing the comparison, they will perform poorly and may even drown.

You can think of WORK SUPPORT as all the things an enterprise puts into place so that work execution can be as effective and efficient as possible. It's a series of usually permanently implemented interventions provided by the company to support accomplishing work at various levels. You would not, for example, send an engineer out to do his or her work without the needed technological tools, management support, skills, training, and so forth. You would not decide on a core process for an assembly line without the latest hardware or software to support it. Neither would you think of forming your business unit level without objectives, strategies, mission/vision, and the like. These, and other work facilitation needs, are all aspects of work support and, when done or provided well, help create and maintain a healthy organization. By contrast, if you decide to ignore these support considerations, provide them at minimal levels, or don't continuously attend to them, you must accept that performance will not be at the levels you desire as an enterprise or for the customers you serve.

Work Support also applies to decisions governing the acquisition and retention of appropriate personnel. Just pay an engineer minimum wage and see what effect that has on your entire enterprise.

Every fair-sized business will require varying degrees of organizational support. Operationally, the administration of these support items usually manifests itself in departments (e.g., Human Resources, Labor Relations, etc.) that coordinate/ deliver such support. Other factors are directly in the hands of management (e.g., hiring); still others, by workers with one another or by teams (e.g., quality circles). You might have or need a Human Resources group to handle support related to hiring, training, career development, performance review and benefits, all of which support work execution. You would not want—though most enterprises do—to determine the scope and provision for such support without knowing the scope and purpose of the work to be executed. That is why we emphasize first defining and aligning work execution. Only then can you define, provide for, and improve the work support.

As it turns out, for all the complexities that support can involve—and there are many—identifying support needs and problems is rather easy when you use the Language of Work. That's because we use the same Work Formula for work execution as we do for work support; thus alignment is assured. We have, as well, arranged work support needs as they relate to business units, core processes, jobs, and work groups. For example, Figure 22 shows the work support interventions that are typically needed at the jobs level:

TYPICAL WORK SUPPORT: JOB LEVEL

INPUTS	CONDITIONS	PROCESS STEPS	OUTPUTS	CONSEQUENCES	FEEDBACK
CLIENT NEEDS & RESOURCES	*WORK INFLUENCES*	*WORK METHODS*	*JOB DELIVERABLES*	*INDIVIDUAL RESULTS*	*CONFIRMATIONS & SELF ADJUSTMENT*
1. Assignments 2. Boss/Organization 3. Equipment/ Facilities 4. Goals & Objectives 5. Identified Client Needs 6. Job Description 7. Strategy	1. Attributes 2. Benefits/Pay 3. Budget 4. Ergonomics 5. Employee Handbook 6. Ethics 7. Policies 8. Safety 9. Schedule 10. Workload	1. Career Development Plan 2. Documentation 3. Performance Improvement Interventions 4. Skill Maint./Devel. 5. Succession Planning 6. Work Flow 7. Work Tools	1. Job Models 2. Individual unit: • Knowledge • Products • Services	1. Customer Satisfaction 2. Job Satisfaction 3. Personal Satisfaction 4. Ties to Work Group	1. Dialogue 2. Internal Client Evaluations 3. Performance Appraisal 4. Rewards & Recognition 5. Turnover

Figure 22

You see listed a number of provisions to support execution of jobs. For example, for process steps you find such items as:

1. Career Development Plan
2. Documentation
3. Performance Improvement Interventions
4. Skill Maintenance/Development
5. Succession Planning
6. Work Flow
7. Work Tools

Having support designated as work flows and work tools would obviously help better execute job processes, use of inputs, adherence to governance, and promotion of feedback. This is also true of provisions for maintaining job skills, such as training, and other performance improvement interventions.

As it turns out, for all the complexities that organizational support can involve—and there are many—identifying organizational support needs and problems is rather easy.

On a more long-term basis, when the enterprise provides career development opportunities, it supports long-term commitment to the workforce and management so that employees are less likely to jump ship. As you review the various interventions of work support at the job level, you can see that these and others need to be constantly attended to if you are sustain a healthy organization. This is what we mean by cultural due diligence—to pay continuous attention to the work environment.

Figure 23 shows what we refer to and use as Work Support Matrix. It's a summary of most of the things that need to be attended to for an enterprise to be healthy. It's organized around the four work execution levels on the vertical axis, and on the horizontal axis, the six elements that comprise the Work Formula. Thus, at the intersection of these axes are listed the kinds of interventions that need to be in place and attended to. You can add others or tailor the matrix as it would best apply to your enterprise's specific work environment. Note that each box is labeled with a reference number (e.g., B2) to provide an easy reference to a set of interventions at a given work level (i.e., 2 is for core processes) and work

WORK SUPPORT MATRIX

PERFORMANCE INTERNATIONAL

.... The Healthy Organization

	INPUTS	CONDITIONS	PROCESS STEPS	OUTPUTS	CONSEQUENCES	FEEDBACK
	STRATEGY & BUS. PLANS	CULTURE / CONTROLS	ADMINISTRATIVE SYSTEMS	BUSINESS DELIVERABLES	BUSINESS RESULTS	BUSINESS MEASUREM./EVALUAT.
BUSINESS UNIT	1. Competitive Advantage 2. Customer Needs 3. Driving Force 4. Mission/vision 5. Strategic Plan (including goals & objectives) **1A**	1. Budget 2. Competition 3. Decision Authority 4. Governance 5. Methods of Change 6. Organizational Units/Functions 7. Regulations **1B**	1. Consistency of operation 2. Degree of centralization/ decentralization 3. Flexibility 4. Linkages/Interactions 5. Organizational Hierarchy **1C**	1. Business Unit Model 2. Business Plan • Knowledge • Products • Services **1D**	1. Marketshare 2. Measures of Success 3. Public Relations 4. Satisfaction of Customers 5. Satisfaction of Stakeholders **1E**	1. Measures of Success 2. Reaction/Requests of Stakeholders/Clients 3. Reputation 4. ROI **1F**
	PROCESS RESOURCES	REGULATIONS/ POLICIES	TECHNOLOGIES (SOFT & HARD)	PROCESS DELIVERABLES	PROCESS RESULTS	CONFIRMATIONS & CORRECTIONS
CORE PROCESSES	1. Individual & Work Group Needs • Equipment • Raw Materials • Intellectual Knowledge 2. Strategy **2A**	1. External Regulations 2. Internal Policies 3. Professional Ethics 4. Professional Standards **2B**	1. Hardware Technologies 2. Knowledge Transfer Mechanisms 3. Management Facilitation 4. Software 5. Systems Approach 6. Schedule **2C**	1. Core Process Model 2. Process • Knowledge • Products • Services **2D**	1. Product or Service • Cost • Delivery • Quality • Quantity **2E**	1. Continuous Improvements 2. Management Reinforcement 3. Measurements 4. Quality Checks 5. Schedules **2F**
	CLIENT NEEDS & RESOURCES	WORK INFLUENCES	WORK METHODS	JOB DELIVERABLES	INDIVIDUAL RESULTS	CONFIRMATIONS & SELF ADJUSTMENT
JOBS	1. Assignments 2. Boss/Organization 3. Equipment/Facilities 4. Goals & Objectives 5. Identified Client Needs 6. Job Description 7. Strategy **3A**	1. Attributes 2. Benefits/Pay 3. Budget 4. Ergonomics 5. Employee Handbook 6. Ethics 7. Policies 8. Safety 9. Schedule 10. Workload **3B**	1. Career Development Plan 2. Documentation 3. Performance Improve- ment Interventions 4. Skill Maint./Devel 5. Succession Planning 6. Work Flow 7. Work Tools **3C**	1. Job Models 2. Individual unit • Knowledge • Products • Services **3D**	1. Customer Satisfaction 2. Job Satisfaction 3. Personal Satisfaction 4. Ties to Work Group **3E**	1. Dialogue 2. Internal Client Evaluations 3. Performance Appraisal 4. Rewards & Recognition 5. Turnover **3F**
	CLIENT NEEDS & RESOURCES	VALUES & PRACTICES	INTERFACE/ RELATIONSHIPS	WORK GROUP DELIVERABLES	WORK GROUP RESULTS	MANAGEMENT/TEAM INFORMATION SYSTEM
WORK GROUPS	1. Business Needs 2. Knowledge 3. Orientation 4. Partners 5. Personnel 6. Projects 7. Strategy **4A**	1. Attributes 2. Budget/Funds 3. Conflict Resolution 4. Culture 5. Decision Authority 6. Ethics 7. Mgmt/Leadership Practices & Expect. 8. Other Group Practices 9. Schedule **4B**	1. Management System 2. Partnerships 3. Performance Improve- ment Interventions 4. Personnel Selection 5. Skill Maint./ Devel 6. Workflow 7. Work Group Ties **4C**	1. Work Group Models 2. Plans • Knowledge • Products • Services **4D**	1. Client Retention 2. Goal Consistency Across Units 3. Repeat Business 4. Reputation 5. Teamwork **4E**	1. Continuous Improvements 2. Facilitation Methods 3. Information Systems 4. Measurements 5. Meetings **4F**

© 1997 Performance International

Figure 23

element (B is for conditions). These reference numbers become useful when assessments are conducted about how effective the organization is in providing specific work support and which need improvement to enhance work execution. This is further explained in the *Managing Model* book.

Generally, one of the best and easiest opportunities to utilize the Work Support Matrix is to do assessments of work support needs while initially modeling work at the four levels of work execution. One should also conduct ongoing periodic assessments as the enterprise goes about its daily business. Thus, at the end of any session in which you have modeled business unit, core processes, jobs, or work group models, you can ask questions and make observations that assess current and missing work support. For example, when we have completed the facilitation of a job model, we ask the assembled group of exemplary performers, "What it is that the enterprise could do better to support the work you trying to accomplish as depicted in the job model you just defined?" In other words, while the work itself is clear and agreed to in the minds of this group of workers (and/or managers), we are asking what else could be done or what could be done better? For example, the "verbatim" answers, as we call them, illustrated in Figure 24, identify trends about what work support should be attended too.

> Generally, the best and easiest way to utilize the Work Support Matrix is do assessments of organizational support needs while initially modeling work at the four levels of work execution.

"In A Perfect World" Verbatim: (sample comments at different work execution levels)		
Work Level	**Verbatim Comment Made by Workers**	**Organizational Support Category**
1A5	Strategic Plan needs updating	Strategic Plan
3C7	Better templates needed for boilerplate	Work Tools
3C7	Outdated templates	Work Tools
4A3	Reason to attend orientation needed	Orientation
4A3	Post-orientation checklist needed	Orientation
4A3	Orientation: schedule, invitation	Orientation
2C2	Better database	Documentation
3F1	Communication with network of attorneys needed	Dialogue
3A2, 3C6,4C1,4B7	Access to Exec Director needed	Management Facilitation
3B10	Attorneys feel overloaded	Workload
3A1	Pro bono attorneys want more say in assignments	Assignments
1B3	Clear lines of responsibility/authority needed	Decision Authority
(continues)		

Figure 24

Verbatims function as an ancillary form of data-gathering during modeling. An attentive facilitator will note on flipchart paper comments and concerns by individuals about what's not being adequately supported and save the sheets for future inclusion with the verbatims collected at the end of modeling sessions. Additionally, as the models are shared with others in the enterprise for their buy-in, you can elicit their verbatims that indicate what needs better support in the business. That old standby of annually asking employees what could be done better in the business can now be summarized on the Work Support Matrix, then judged for its impact on work execution in a much more meaningful and communicative way for management to act upon.

These sources of verbatims will accumulate from one modeling session to another and as they are contributed when the models are shared. You will be systematically gathering the work support data that needs to be acted upon. You will begin to note trends and frequency of certain comments and code them to the Work Support Matrix. In our consulting practice, we use a version of our Work Support Excel software spreadsheet to enter the data and sort it for trends. We then display the results as illustrated in Figure 25 (for AITS).

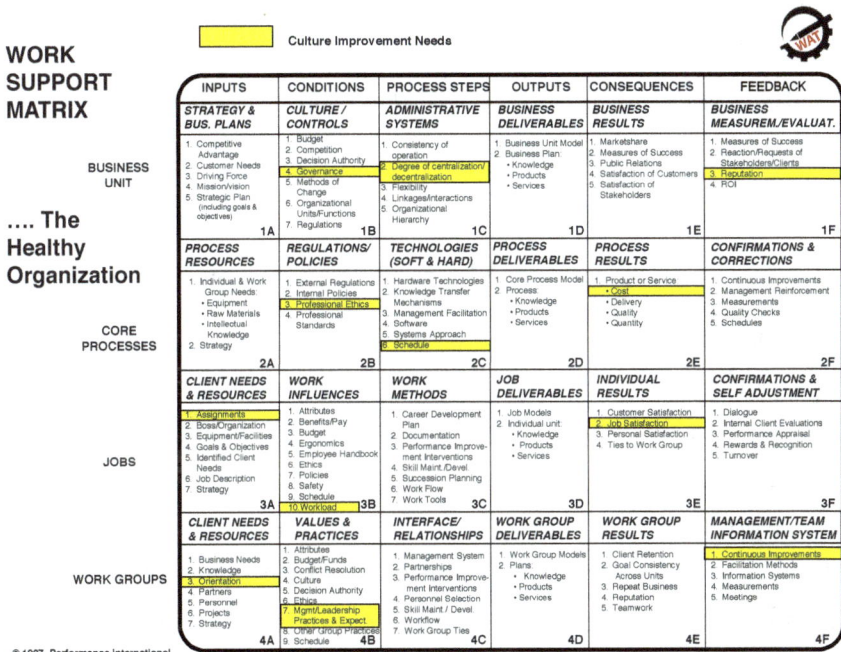

WORK SUPPORT MATRIX

.... The Healthy Organization

Culture Improvement Needs

	INPUTS	CONDITIONS	PROCESS STEPS	OUTPUTS	CONSEQUENCES	FEEDBACK
	STRATEGY & BUS. PLANS	**CULTURE / CONTROLS**	**ADMINISTRATIVE SYSTEMS**	**BUSINESS DELIVERABLES**	**BUSINESS RESULTS**	**BUSINESS MEASUREM/EVALUAT.**
BUSINESS UNIT	1. Competitive Advantage 2. Customer Needs 3. Driving Force 4. Mission/vision 5. Strategic Plan (including goals & objectives) **1A**	1. Budget 2. Competition 3. Decision Authority 4. Governance 5. Methods of Change 6. Organizational Units/Functions 7. Regulations **1B**	1. Consistency of operation 2. Degree of centralization/ decentralization 3. Flexibility 4. Linkages/Interactions 5. Organizational Hierarchy **1C**	1. Business Unit Model 2. Business Plan: • Knowledge • Products • Services **1D**	1. Marketshare 2. Measures of Success 3. Public Relations 4. Satisfaction of Customers 5. Satisfaction of Stakeholders **1E**	1. Measures of Success 2. Reaction/Requests of Stakeholders/Clients 3. Reputation 4. ROI **1F**
	PROCESS RESOURCES	**REGULATIONS/ POLICIES**	**TECHNOLOGIES (SOFT & HARD)**	**PROCESS DELIVERABLES**	**PROCESS RESULTS**	**CONFIRMATIONS & CORRECTIONS**
CORE PROCESSES	1. Individual & Work Group Needs: • Equipment • Raw Materials • Intellectual Knowledge 2. Strategy **2A**	1. External Regulations 2. Internal Policies 3. Professional Ethics 4. Professional Standards **2B**	1. Hardware Technologies 2. Knowledge Transfer Mechanisms 3. Management Facilitation 4. Software 5. Systems Approach 6. Schedule **2C**	1. Core Process Model 2. Process: • Knowledge • Products • Services **2D**	1. Product or Service • Cost • Delivery • Quality • Quantity **2E**	1. Continuous Improvements 2. Management Reinforcement 3. Measurements 4. Quality Checks 5. Schedules **2F**
	CLIENT NEEDS & RESOURCES	**WORK INFLUENCES**	**WORK METHODS**	**JOB DELIVERABLES**	**INDIVIDUAL RESULTS**	**CONFIRMATIONS & SELF ADJUSTMENT**
JOBS	1. Assignments 2. Boss/Organization 3. Equipment/Facilities 4. Goals & Objectives 5. Identified Client Needs 6. Job Description 7. Strategy **3A**	1. Attributes 2. Benefits/Pay 3. Budget 4. Ergonomics 5. Employee Handbook 6. Ethics 7. Policies 8. Safety 9. Schedule 10. Workload **3B**	1. Career Development Plan 2. Documentation 3. Performance Improve-ment Interventions 4. Skill Maint./Devel. 5. Succession Planning 6. Work Flow 7. Work Tools **3C**	1. Job Models 2. Individual unit: • Knowledge • Products • Services **3D**	1. Customer Satisfaction 2. Job Satisfaction 3. Personal Satisfaction 4. Ties to Work Group **3E**	1. Dialogue 2. Internal Client Evaluations 3. Performance Appraisal 4. Rewards & Recognition 5. Turnover **3F**
	CLIENT NEEDS & RESOURCES	**VALUES & PRACTICES**	**INTERFACE/ RELATIONSHIPS**	**WORK GROUP DELIVERABLES**	**WORK GROUP RESULTS**	**MANAGEMENT/TEAM INFORMATION SYSTEM**
WORK GROUPS	1. Business Needs 2. Knowledge 3. Orientation 4. Partners 5. Personnel 6. Projects 7. Strategy **4A**	1. Attributes 2. Budget/Funds 3. Conflict Resolution 4. Culture 5. Decision Authority 6. Ethics 7. Mgmt/Leadership Practices & Expect. 8. Other Group Practices 9. Schedule **4B**	1. Management System 2. Partnerships 3. Performance Improve-ment Interventions 4. Personnel Selection 5. Skill Maint./Devel. 6. Workflow 7. Work Group Ties **4C**	1. Work Group Models 2. Plans: • Knowledge • Products • Services **4D**	1. Client Retention 2. Goal Consistency Across Units 3. Repeat Business 4. Reputation 5. Teamwork **4E**	1. Continuous Improvements 2. Facilitation Methods 3. Information Systems 4. Measurements 5. Meetings **4F**

© 1997 Performance International

Figure 25

Above you can see color-coded areas of work support on the matrix showing needed attention in the AITS enterprise, according to the verbatims that we collected. Those coded in yellow were for improvements that stem from an analysis of the verbatims in terms of their frequency and what items of work support (e.g., lack of good job descriptions) need improvement or are simply lacking (e.g., career development opportunities). The matrix becomes part of an easily grasped report to management showing where the organization is weakest and how its weaknesses impact work execution and client satisfaction.

The Work Support Matrix can also be used, after modeling has long been completed, to look systematically at what support does or doesn't exist and how it can be made better. It is used as a kind of checklist of support items to be periodically reviewed by management and others (e.g., an HR Department). The positive effect of this will be to keep work support needs in mind for a healthy organization. Further guidelines and description of Work Support analysis is provided in *The Managing Model* of *The Work Trilogy*.

Aligning Human Relations

Work, as it relates to human relations, is exactly what it implies. It is, perhaps, the scourge of many an enterprise and certainly affects work execution on many dimensions, from internal relations to client satisfaction. The enterprise that fails to monitor and assure positive human relations will suffer negative consequences. Here, we will see the many dimensions of human relations and learn how to account for its impact and do something about it in a positive way.

The first thing to recognize is that human relations issues occur on all levels of work execution, not just the individual job level. As part of the Business Model, we represent these in the following matrix as keyed to the four levels of work execution in Figure 26.

As you review the Human Relations Matrix you may be surprised to note that most of what is listed must be provided by the business management. While human relations is, of course, an individual personality and relationship component that should be the responsibility of individuals, we know that much of what the

HUMAN RELATIONS MATRIX

	INPUTS	CONDITIONS	PROCESS STEPS	OUTPUTS	CONSEQUENCES	FEEDBACK
BUSINESS UNIT	**STRATEGY & BUS. PLANS** 1. New Business Ideas Encouraged 2. Customer/Client Input Requested 3. Communications Sought 4. Realistic Strategic Plans **1A**	**CULTURE / CONTROLS** 1. Positive Culture 2. Equal Opportunity 3. Friendly 4. Personal Compliance with Guidelines 5. Adherence to Contracts 6. Equitable Application of Compensation 7. Career Development & Advancement Equity **1B**	**MARKET SYSTEMS** 1. Responsive processes 2. Cooperation 3. Encouraged **1C**	**BUSINESS DELIVERABLES** 1. Quality Work Encouraged in Products and Services **1D**	**BUSINESS RESULTS** 1. Positive Reputation 2. Repeat Business 3. Customer Is Right **1E**	**BUSINESS MEASUREM./EVALUAT.** 1. Positive Client Reaction 2. Bottom-up Information Flow 3. Management Listens & Responds **1F**
CORE PROCESSES	**RESOURCES** 1. Positive/Constructive Worker/Manager Input 2. Resources Provided **2A**	**REGULATIONS/ POLICIES** 1. Compliance Sought 2. Rules/regulations Followed 3. Ethics Required **2B**	**TECHNOLOGIES (SOFT & HARD)** 1. Process Followed 2. Changes Are Possible 3. Time Is Important 4. Innovation Is Okay 5. Value Is Added 6. Sabotage Is Not Okay **2C**	**PRODUCTS & SERVICES** 1. Outputs Are Supported/Important **2D**	**PROCESS RESULTS** 1. Quality of Work Encouraged 2. No Delays **2E**	**CONFIRMATIONS & CORRECTION** 1. Feedback Encouraged 2. Suggestions Made 3. Feedback Sought **2F**
JOBS	**CLIENT NEEDS & RESOURCES** 1. Selection By Skill & Experience 2. Client Attended To 3. Resources Available 4. Mgmt. Information Available 5. Clear expectations **3A**	**WORK INFLUENCES** 1. Clear Productivity Expectations 2. Positive Environment 3. Policies Followed 4. Pay Equity 5. Ethics 6. Job Growth **3B**	**WORK METHODS** 1. Processes Followed 2. Quality Expectations 3. Continuous Learning 4. Assignment By Skill & Ability 5. Personal Productivity 6. Ideas Encouraged 7. "Not Blaming Others" **3C**	**PRODUCTS & SERVICES** 1. Quality Outputs 2. Valuing others' output and input **3D**	**INDIVIDUAL RESULTS** 1. Client Valued/Right 2. Individual Valued 3. Product/Service Valued 4. Individual Rewarded **3E**	**CONFIRMATIONS & SELF ADJUSTMENT** 1. Information Encouraged 2. Reinforcement Given 3. Useful Performance Review 4. Questions Asked/Answers Given 5. Productivity Information Provided **3F**
WORK GROUPS	**CLIENT NEEDS & RESOURCES** 1. Team Input Sought 2. Client Attended To 3. Resources Used 4. Group Needs/ Requests Sought **4A**	**VALUES & PRACTICES** 1. Clear Productivity Expectations 2. Positive Environment Supported 3. Policies Followed 4. Ethics Required **4B**	**INTERFACE/ RELATIONSHIPS** 1. Teamwork Used 2. Quality Work Sought 3. Defined Processes Followed 5. Productivity Achieved 6. Continuous Learning Expected **4C**	**PRODUCTS & SERVICES** 1. Collaborative Output 2. Quality Products/ Services Produced **4D**	**GROUP RESULTS** 1. Group Rewarded 2. Client Valued/Right 3. Individual Valued 4. Group Satisfaction Encouraged **4E**	**MANAGEMENT/TEAM INFORMATION SYSTEM** 1. Positive Client Reaction 2. Information Shared 3. Individuals Get Along 4. Information Flows 5. Questions Asked/Answers Given **4F**

Figure 26

individual does is encouraged or discouraged because of the business atmosphere and the culture of work. This is what is usually meant by a "positive culture."

Businesses that attend to the items found in the Human Resources Matrix are the ones that people like to work in and that customers find satisfaction from. Therefore, it is incumbent upon the business to constantly seek and plan for needed adjustments in its human relations goals and practice. In the same way that we suggested scanning your enterprise for Work Support, so you too can scan, attend to, and align human relations issues with their effects on work execution. Positive human relations don't occur by chance; they take careful planning. The matrix will help you both with planning and evaluation of attainment.

Aligning Financial Support

The financial means and degree of support provided to operate a business obviously impact effectiveness. Budget influences all levels and other layers of work. The question is, "What aspects of financial support need be attended to?" The answer is business specific, of course, so you will be using, as with other layers of work, a matrix of financial factors that you will need to tailor to your business and scan on a continuing basis.

The Financial Support Matrix is represented in Figure 27.

FINANCIAL SUPPORT MATRIX

.... *The Financially Sound Organization*

	INPUTS	CONDITIONS	PROCESS STEPS	OUTPUTS	CONSEQUENCES	FEEDBACK
BUSINESS UNIT	**STRATEGY AND FINANCIAL PLANS** 1. Valuation 2. Customer Revenues 3. Cost Enhancements 4. Assets/Liabilities/ Equity 5. Market 6. Owner Investments 7. Secure Financing 8. Working Capital 9. Identifying Client Needs 1A	**GOVERNANCE COMPLIANCE** 1. Capital Budget 2. Risk vs. Return Assessment 3. Forecasting/Financial Planning 4. Interest Rates 5. GAAP 6. IFRB ??? 7. Fiscal Compliance 8. Industry Sector 9. External Infrastructure 10. Environmental Impact 11. Taxes 1B	**SYSTEMS COSTS** 1. Cash Management 2. Treasury 3. Purchasing 4. Customer Acquisition 5. Sales Orders 6. Admin. Sys. Costs 1C	**BUSINESS OUTPUT COSTS** 1. Profit 2. Revenues 3. Direct Costs 4. Operating Expenses 5. Capital Expenditures 6. Accounts Receivables 7. Inventory 8. Payables 9. Net Cash Flows 1D	**BUSINESS RESULTS** 1. ROI 2. Net Profit 3. EDITDA 4. Gross Margin 5. Cost of Capital 6. ROA 7. Safety 8. Environmental Impact 9. Public/Client Relations 1E	**BUSINESS MEASUM'TS./ EVALUATION** 1. Valuation 2. Cash Flows 3. Return On Assets (ROA) 4. Return On Income 5. Return On Sales 6. Business EDITDA/Fundamentals 7. Dividends 8. Stock Value 9. Customer Value 1F

CORE PROCESSES	**PROCESS RESOURCES COSTS**
	1. Company Cash
	2. Capital Raised
	3. Leverage
	4. Facilities & Equipment
	5. Raw Materials
	6. Intellectual Knowledge
	2A
		REGULATIONS/ POLICIES
		1. GAAP
		2. State/Federal Laws
		3. Contracts
		4. Gross Margins
		5. Hourly Rate
		6. Benefits
		7. Shrinkage
		8. Time Value of Money
		9. Taxes
		10. Professional Standards
		2B
			TECHNOLOGIES (SOFT & HARD)
			1. Sales
			2. Marketing
			3. Advertising
			4. Production
			5. Service Delivery Tech.
			  • Practice
			  • Process
			6. General Accounting
			7. Treasury
			8. Accounts Payable
			9. Accounts Receivable
			10. Inventory
			11. Payroll
			12. Taxes
			13. Cash Management
			2C
				PROCESS DELIVERABLES
				1. Sales Income
				2. Gross Margins
				3. Operating Expenses
				4. Inventory
				5. Accounts Receivable
				6. Accounts Payable
				7. Capital Expenditures
				2D
					PROCESS RESULTS
					1. Gross Margin
					2. Profitability
					3. Net Cash Flow
					4. Earnings
					2E
						CONFIRMATIONS & CORRECTIONS
						1. Bad Debt
						2. A/R Turnover
						3. Collection Period
						4. Financial Statements
						2F

JOBS	**INDIVIDUAL RESOURCES COSTS** 1. Product Price 2. Hourly Rate 3. Estimated Time 4. Cost Factors 5. Generate Income 6. Labor Kinds 7. Tools & Materials for Indiv.ls 8. Benefits 3A	**INDIVIDUAL COMPLIANCE** 1. Cash flow goals 2. Daily Income 3. Cost of Materials 4. Safety 5. Workload 3B	**INDIVIDUAL WORK METHODS** 1. Assembly 2. Distribution 3. Service Delivery 4. Skills/Maint Dev. Costs 5. Work Tools 6. Succession Planing 7. Career Devel m Costs 8. Personnel Selection 3C	**JOB DELIVERABLES** 1. Customer 2. Income 3. Reduce Costs 4. Identify New Revenue Stream 5. Preserve Assets 6. Accurate Paperwork 7. Efficient Systems 8. Sales Orders 9. Invoices Paid 3D	**INDIVIDUAL RESULTS** 1. Cost/benefit 2. Units produced 3. Sufficient Work for day 4. Product Quality Maintained 3E	**INDIVIDUAL MEASUM.TS & IMPROVM.** 1. 360 Cost appraisal 2. Cost/benefit analysis 3. Employee value/salary 4. Benefits 5. Personal Satisfaction 3F
WORK GROUPS/ MANAGEMENT	**GROUP RESOURCES COSTS** 1. Product Price 2. Group Rate 3. Estimated Time 4. Cost Factors 5. Generate Income 6. Labor Mix 7. Tools & Materials for Groups 4A	**GROUP COMPLIANCE** 1. Cash flow goals 2. Daily Income 3. Cost of Materials 4B	**GROUP WORK METHODS** 1. Assembly 2. Distribution 3. Service Delivery 4. Mgmt System Costs 4C	**WORK GROUP DELIVERABLES** 1. Customer 2. Income 3. Reduce Costs 4. Identify New Revenue Stream 5. Preserve Assets 6. Accurate Paperwork 7. Efficient Systems 8. Sales Orders 9. Invoices Paid 4D	**INDIVIDUAL RESULTS** 1. Cost/benefit 2. Units produced 3. Sufficient Work 4E	**GROUP/MGMT. MEASUM.TS & IMPROVM** 1. 360 Cost appraisal 2. Cost/benefit analysis 3. Employee value/salary 4. Group Satisfaction 5. Management Satisfaction 4F

© 2014 Performance International

Figure 27

As with the other work layer matrices, in this matrix you find the identification of financial factors that influence work execution, standards, work support, and human relations. Most relate, as would be expected, to work execution, but it is important to realize that the other three layers of work are also in need of financial support. You may pay workers, for example, an adequate and accepted wage, but if you can't provide the quality of equipment needed, their work will be negatively affected. The discussion of this matrix, keyed to your company, will reveal valuable insights into how your workforce views its challenges and needs.

Summary

We intentionally provided additional detail in the discussion of the Work Support Matrix as it provides the general guidelines in the use of any of the other matrices. The first thing to do is tailor each matrix to your business environment. Doing so is not just to make it business specific, but also to garner valuable insight into how your employees view the impact of the various aspects of each layers of work. As with work level modeling, you will find that the product is useful for the various reasons we have described. You will also find that the discussions that accompany modeling and refinement of work matrices provide numerous insights and useful information from the work force. This alone will result in some improvements.

Following the tailoring process, you will then apply the matrices. This takes two forms. The first is the act of setting standards, identifying work support, human relations issues, and needed financial support. These typically occur following modeling of business unit, core processes, jobs, and work groups. The second form—and repeated on a continuous basis—is that of "scanning" work layer support and its impact on work execution. Both of these forms of applying the matrices are illustrated and described in further detail in *The Managing Model* of *The Work Trilogy*. You are encouraged to engage in setting and scanning for all four dimensions of work layers.

Chapter 9

Achieving Continuous Improvement

Business survival depends on continuous improvement from within. In this concluding chapter we show you, an executive, how to utilize the LoW for continuous improvement. We first address having a more successful approach to continuous improvement. Secondly, we demonstrate how to promote a mindset that encourages everyone in the organization to self-improve. This is a mindset that focuses on work—not psychology, politics, or other extraneous rabbit trails—

> We conclude *The Business Model* with what it takes to assure that the business remains efficient, effective, and open to change, because change is inevitable if a business is to survive in an ever-changing economic climate.

that naturally occurs when work is understood, defined, and implemented with the LoW. Adopting the Language of Work is a significant step in the right direction.

The leading approaches to continuous improvement have hitherto been programmatic—that is, purchased by management and installed in the organization by internal or external consultants. These "programs" instill methods of improvement, while also creating organizational centers and activities that encourage, publicize, reward and indeed spur such improvements. These programs are add-ons to the current work being accomplished and may be effective in the short term, but cannot be maintained because they add to the work load. They are not part of the way employees view their work. They are generally seen as what management wants employees to do. We have come to believe that employees would naturally make improvements if they knew how and had the means and freedom to do so.

What if continuous improvement were a natural extension of doing the work? Would continuous improvement then be more likely to occur regularly as compared to programs that rise and ebb in direct relation to management interest and encouragement? We recognize that programmatic approaches can be useful. We also know that it would be desirable to have improvement naturally occur as part of ongoing work implementation. We address both of these below. We end by showing how the LoW promotes *real* continuous improvement as a natural extension of defining and organizing work using the LoW Work Formula.

Enhancing Legacy Programs for Continuous Improvement

There are three approaches we have developed based on the LoW that are worthy adjuncts to your existing programs for work improvement. They are Performance Appraisal (yes, a continuous improvement program), Dots on Model, and Work Scans. This is an introduction to each of these, as they are further explained in the other two books of *The Work Trilogy*. You need not delve into the details; only know enough to provide support. Instead, managers and workers will handle the implementation itself.

Performance Review/Appraisal Programs

We can almost hearing you saying to yourself, "Not another Performance Review program!" If you have been an executive for very long, you have experienced the negative side of such programs far more than the positive. Certainly the authors, in their own work experiences in the six companies they have worked for can't recall any program that was particularly effective. None resulted in substantive work improvement. As often as not, both managers and workers eventually abandoned these efforts or filled out the forms reluctantly with little or no follow-up.

Still, we intuitively know that periodic reviewing of one's performance has to be done. There are legal reasons, of course, but it is also helpful to reassure workers that some things are going right and that managers are confident in the work of those being managed. Even your direct reports need such reviews for the same reasons. Unfortunately, because until now there has not been a quick and reliable way to define performance (work), most performance appraisal systems are based on pop psychology, attitude descriptions, or the ability to play well with others. If your program is stronger than that, congratulations. Fortunately, the LoW makes performance reviews effective precisely because it ensures work is defined in a behavioral way. One need only determine between parties (management and worker) if that definition of the work is being followed or needs improvement.

A brief overview will hopefully convince you that the first level of continuous work improvement can be an effective performance review program.

The LoW definition of work, especially at the job level, is highly understandable, functional, and consistent with achieving work organization, alignment, and transparency. This guarantees success in achieving continuous improvement and making changes in work. Performance review focuses on work execution and support—nothing else. The evaluation is conducted not against a wish list, but precisely in terms of *effect* is to be achieved (outputs and consequences), and what *causes* these to be achieved in terms of inputs, conditions, process steps, and feedback. Thus in reviewing a worker, manager, and even an executive's work, those managing such individuals can evaluate the work produced. If deliverables are not being delivered, a meaningful and specifically directed discussion can occur covering where the difficulties arose and what might be done to change or improve such work. And this can be done constructively reaching solutions, rather than placing blame.

Furthermore, information from these discussions (performance reviews) can be fed into internal organizations (such as training, improvement centers, organizational effectiveness, career development, leadership, quality initiatives, etc.) for analysis. The data serve as the input from both management and employees that is needed in order to devise meaningful solutions fostering system wide improvements. In addition, the meaningful worker-boss discussion has resulted in micro improvements even before it gets to other work improvement entities in the company, such as training. You are encouraged to review the more specific details on performance review in *The Managing Model* and *The Working Model* books of this series.

Dots on Models

One of the most difficult challenges executives face is knowing where to place energy and resources for making improvements. Our society tries to depend on data, but data is only persuasive some of the time. Our society depends on debate and argumentation to arrive at good conclusions. Yet these too can mislead, because the loudest voice too often wins.

The Language of Work overcomes both these problems by beginning every project with a definition of the work. While process engineering can take months and exhaust all players in the process, we can and do define core processes in less than two days. Once we have agreement (albeit at a very high level) on the actual work, then we can "get into people's heads" with a fascinating tool: Dots on Models.

An example comes from our work with resolving issues that were revealed after a natural disaster. The emergency response system used by an electric utility had failed…and the failure meant that people were without power for more than twelve days.

Complicating the situation exponentially was that 87 different towns (each with a different mayor and city council) were affected—and the power utility shared a distribution network with other utilities and cable, Internet, TV, and telephone providers. Various federal, state, and local agencies had to find ways to work together to get the power back on, each with its own perspective and needs on the overall problem. Before the LoW was utilized to define the core processes, identifying (through a color code) where each agency had a role, there was significant finger-pointing. When a group representing each of the various parties and agencies assembled, their shared Core Process Model was reviewed with slight edits. Then each agency was given five adhesive dots to place on the process to identify the main areas where problems existed.

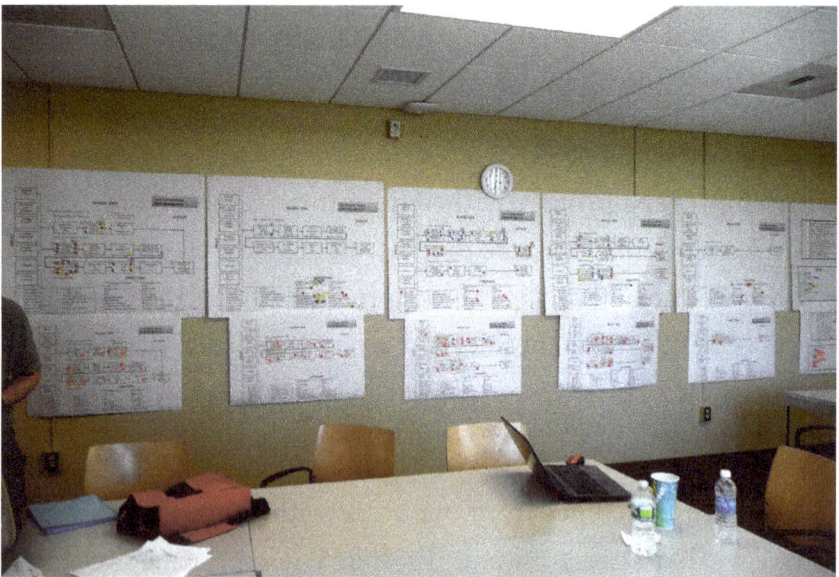

As a result, participants quickly saw the areas most people thought were problem areas. Amazingly, each agency identified the area they were most responsible for resolving. Many times this realization prompted a policy change or a directive from management. There were further discussions, but all participants left the meeting after one day with an action list and a deadline.

While this is a more complex example of work improvement involving many different work groups from different companies and agencies, it is not as dissimilar to having to improve internally a single team, work group, or core process. Dots on Models, one of the Work Analytic Tools of the LoW, can be very effective in determining where the problems are. Descriptions of what needs improvement can then be focused in reality. Discussion on the best means for resolving those ends then takes place based in a consensus environment. Solutions are analyzed in terms of cost, disruption, and risk, rather than being a source of contention. The details for modeling and doing Dots on Models are provided in *The Managing Model.*

Work Scans

If it can be said that a performance review is the measure of the work health of an individual, then a Work Scan is a valuable measure of the health of an enterprise. It is the responsibility of executive management to assure a healthy work environment. Until now, there has been no systematic way of measuring and improving organizational health. Employee engagement scores and other fads are attempts to achieve this goal...but they are likely to miss the mark by not having agreement on the fundamental question: What do we do (deliver, produce, provide) as an organization to achieve our desired consequences?

The LoW Work Scan will go a long ways towards achieving that goal.

Mechanically, Work Scans are best conducted by professionals. Organizational effectiveness, organizational development, HR, training units, or performance technologists—see the International Society for Performance Improvement, ispi.org for details—have the skills in data collection, sorting, classifying, and analyzing data. Still, executives need to have an understanding of work scanning so they can support its installation. So we provide a brief overview. Details are available in *The Managing Model* of this series. Results focusing on the business unit and core processes are the executive arena.

The robustness of the LoW which allows continuous improvement in your organization is not solely about improving work execution at the four levels where work occurs (business unit, core process, individual and work group). There are four **layers** of work you, as an executive, are chiefly responsible for. These four layers support work execution; they often need improvement as well. These four layers can collectively be described as the culture of the organization. As noted previously, the LoW labels them Work Standards, Work Support, Human Relations, and Financial Support. How will you continuously improve these? We suggest you use the LoW Work Analytic Tool known as Work Scans. This has been successfully implemented by several companies and government agencies to improve the culture of their enterprise.

We have found in our continuous improvement work with business that it is highly useful at the end of modeling sessions (while the work is freshly understood and consensus has been achieved), to ask participants a basic question:

In light of what we have just modeled, what could the business (or management) do to make it easier for you to do your work?

This is a fundamental question that elicits word-for-word expressions of what managers and workers feel could be done better. These are not scales of satisfaction/dissatisfaction, nor open-ended questions with no potential for analysis. The verbatim comments that result are the undistilled words of employees. They have not gone through various filters to make them more innocuous or palatable. At the same time, they are useful because they focus on the work. They are classified against a Work Support Matrix to show where comments fall in terms of a healthy organization. These specific work improvement needs can be fed into your quality circle or other already existing work improvement programs. They might be the exclusive purview of the executive team. The tagging of these verbatims to a particular place on a particular matrix, grounded in the execution of work, is what differentiates this method from other ways of making improvements. How to capture, sort, analyze, and solve these work support improvement needs will be further detailed in *The Managing Model*.

Establishing a Mindset for Continuous Work Improvement

The very best way to continuously improve work occurs when the executives, managers, and workers set their individual minds and collective action toward improving work themselves. Unfortunately, there are typically only a few individuals who make this a way of life in their careers. They constantly seek to learn new things, improve on what they already know, request more education and training from the company, pursue a career path, want leadership roles, and participate in almost every opportunity to learn. Any company would love to hire and retain more such people. The problem is, continuous personal and career growth does not come naturally to most people.

The LoW, by clarifying work for everyone through the Work Formula, establishes a vocabulary for discussing work and making it better. The LoW is a version of systems thinking that helps to identify and meet work improvement opportunities. As an executive, you can capitalize on this vocabulary for improvement in your discussions, as well as by prompting managers to act accordingly. Here we will show you a few ways that this is possible.

The authors consulted with a leading high-tech company near the origination of the LoW, around 1992. We were just starting to introduce and facilitate implementation and use of the LoW in several companies. We were subsequently told by some early adopters like the high-tech company mentioned above that they still use it through some of the ways we have introduced in this book. But, they also find the principles of the LoW embedded in their ongoing thinking, discussion, planning, measurement, and execution of work, including work improvement. For example, meetings are often organized on what outputs and consequences are being addressed, followed by reporting, as needed, on actions concerning utilization of inputs, conditions, process steps, and/or feedback. Similarly, planning and problem-solving sessions follow a similar track, and so forth. Many of these are illustrated and described in *The Managing Model.*

To illustrate the Mindset we are suggesting that you can promote by your actions, here is an unsolicited comment from one executive who was recently introduced to the Language of Work:

"I've been building an ops manual, SOPs, and project management tools for my company based on your work formula/

language. It has revolutionized our way of defining processes. One of the reasons I love it is because it overlays on a macro scale as well as a micro level. By micro I mean I've made meeting minute templates that define action items for tasks as well as the conditions, inputs needed, and feedback for the action item output. Maybe I went a little wild applying it, but it's been working great."

There are things you can do to promote this kind of systems thinking, i.e., this kind of mindset. You can encourage your managers, for example, to report to you in these terms, and to help you see the problems they are facing in context of the six elements of the Work Formula. This will, in turn, encourage managers to do so with their workers.

There is a version of this systems thinking when it comes to continuous work improvement that is built into the LoW. It is introduced to managers and workers in the respective books of *The Work Trilogy*. There are two parts to this. The first is promoting an approach that says, "Quality Is Me!" Workers and managers are encouraged to take the very Work Formula that has been used to define their core processes, jobs, and work groups and then use it to measure and identify what needs to improve. They can then make those improvements either on their own, with fellow workers, and with their management (using the LoW as a problem solving technique). This approach builds the continuous improvement muscle of an organization; it provides a common, shared understanding of work that can be measured and continuously made better. When major changes are needed, such as a new technology, the team has the mindset needed to implement them.

A second tool used in establishing the continuous improvement mindset is a Work Analytic Tool we call the Work Improvement Solution Aid. It presents a series of questions linked to the Work Model. It is illustrated and further explained in *The Working Model* and *The Managing Model*. Reviewing it will suggest ways it might be utilized by you, other executives, and managers to improve work continuously and systematically.

What's Next?

After modeling your business using the LoW, you will want to cascade the clarity of work throughout the organization. Thus, given that the Language of Work uses the same work formula at every level of the organization, it can be used by managers to facilitate and workers to implement work. Please refer managers and workers to the following other eBooks of *The Work Trilogy*:

Book 2: *The Managing Model*

Book 3: *The Working Model*

Language of Work Terminology

Continuous Improvement Mindset

The natural extension of the Language of Work to improve work growing out of a fundamental understanding and use of a Work Formula. One of three goals of the Language of Work.

Financial Support Matrix

This matrix extends the application of the Language of Work formula to identify the financials an organization needs to support work execution.

Human Relations Matrix

This matrix extends the Language of Work formula to the areas of human interaction necessary to support work execution.

Language of Work

A systemic, enterprisewide behavioral model, based on the Work Formula, that integrates organizing, managing, implementing, and continuously improving work. In so doing it establishes a way to achieve alignment, transparency, and continuous improvement throughout an organization.

Work Alignment

Use of a Work Formula to ensure that work between different levels is in keeping with the goals and desired consequences of the organization. One of three goals of the Language of Work.

Work Analytic Tools

A variety of ways to use the Work Formula. Can be used to choose approaches for applying the Language of Work formula.

Work Analytics

The process used to analyze work. In the Language of Work, it is the Work Formula.

Work Formula

The six systemic elements that make up work: Inputs, Conditions, Process Steps, Outputs, Consequences, and Feedback.

Work Layer

Those aspects of work that promote and sustain work execution: Standards, Work Support (aka culture), Human Relations, and Financial Support. In the LoW, each of these is represented by a matrix.

Work Level

The Language of Work formula is applied to the four arenas where work is executed: business units, core processes, jobs, and work groups.

Work Matrices

The graphic representation of Work Layers using the Work Formula on one axis and the Levels of Work on the other. Each cell is populated with programs, services, and interventions (or change processes) provided by the organization to support work execution.

Work Models

Graphic flow diagrams based on the elements of the Work Formula. When populated with data from the appropriate work level, they show the work of business units, core processes, jobs, and work groups.

Work Standards Matrix

This matrix extends the Language of Work formula to standards to which work execution should rise in terms of quality, quantity, timeliness, and cost.

Work Support Matrix

The cultural provisions provided by an organization in direct support of work execution at the business unit, core processes, jobs, and work group levels.

Work Transparency

Assuring that the organization's work is clearly defined and understood by everyone at each Work Level and Layer. No secrets in the work. One of three goals of the Language of Work.

Language of Work Implementation Models

The Business Model has been addressed in this eBook. *The Managing Model* and *The Working Model* are addressed in the two other eBooks of *The Work Trilogy*.

The following are the three major Work Implementation Models of the Language of Work. These are followed by a list of Organizational Effectiveness techniques that can use the Language of Work to improve their overall efficiency and effectiveness. You may access definitions, articles, case studies, books, and other information, including certification, at our website: www.performanceinternational.com

Language of Work
The Business Model

For Executives

Work Formula

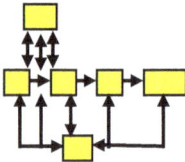

1. **Business Unit Model**
2. **Core Process Models**
3. **Job Models**
4. **Work Group Models**
5. **Work Standards Matrix**
6. **Work Support Matrix**
7. **Human Relations Matrix**
8. **Financial Support Matrix**

TO ACHIEVE:
- **Work Alignment**
- **Transparency**
- **Continuous Improvement**

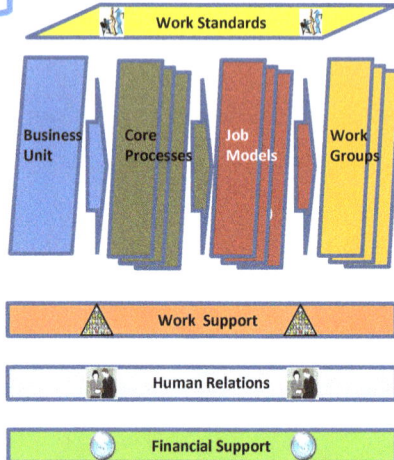

Work Standards

Business Unit | Core Processes | Job Models | Work Groups

Work Support

Human Relations

Financial Support

Language of Work
The Managing Model

For Managers

TO ACHIEVE:
- **Work Facilitation Alignment**
- **Transparency**
- **Continuous Improvement**

9. Planning Work
10. Linking With Other Groups
11. Selecting Employees
12. Job/Work Group Orientation
13. Establishing Systems
14. Assigning Tasks
15. Facilitating Work
16. Reinforcing Work Performance
17. Training & Work Performance
18. Facilitating Change
19. Facilitating Work Support
20. Informing Management
21. Job & Work Group Models
22. Assuring Role Relationships
23. Conducting Meetings
24. Improving Quality
25. Problem Solving
26. Resolving Conflicts
27. Measuring Work
28. Transferring Knowledge
29. Reviewing Performance
30. Career Development

Work Formula

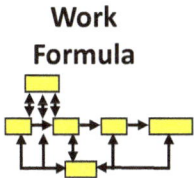

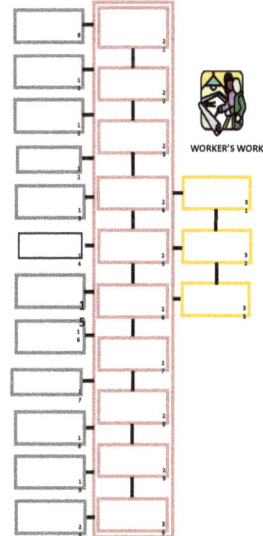

Language of Work

The Working Model

For Individual Worker and Team

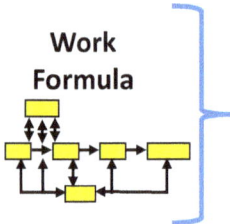

Work Formula

31. **Work Implementation**
32. **Continuous Work Improvement**

TO ACHIEVE:
- **Work Alignment**
- **Transparency**
- **Continuous Improvement**

Organizational Effectiveness interventions that may be enhanced by use of the Language of Work Model:

Language of Work

Organizational Effectiveness

For:
Change Agents,
Performance
Consultants,
Trainers, HR, etc.

Work Formula

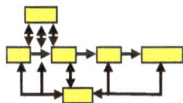

33. **Integrated HR System**
34. **Competency Modeling**
35. **Re-engineering**
36. **Total Quality Management**
37. **Lean**
38. **Reorganization**
39. **Mergers**
40. **Acquisitions**
41. **New Business Start-up**
42. **Downsizing**
43. **Outsourcing**
44. **Expanding Operations**
45. **Training Needs Assessment & Development**
46. **Intervention Selection**
47. **Job Descriptions**
48. **Identifying & Loading Jobs to Core Processes**

TO ACHIEVE:
- **Systems Approac based on LoW**
- **Consistency with LoW Models**

PERFORMANCE INTERNATIONAL

References

Langdon, Danny G. (1995), *The New Language of Work*. Amherst, MA: HRD Press.

Langdon, Danny G. (2000). *Aligning performance: Improving people, systems and organizations*. San Francisco, CA: Jossey-Bass/Pheiffer Publishers.

Langdon, Danny G., Kathleen Whiteside, and Monica McKenna. (1999). *Interventions Resource Guide: 50 Performance Improvement Tools*. San Francisco, CA: Jossey-Bass/Pheiffer Publishers.

Langdon, Danny G., Kathleen Langdon, Johnilee Whiteside, (2014). *Righting the Enterprise – A Primer for Organizing or Reorganizing the Right Way*. Bellingham, Wa: Performance International (free from our website at: http://lnkd.in/d66wnjb or in other formats at: https://www.smashwords.com/books/view/431840

Langdon, Danny G. and Kathleen Langdon. (2018) The Work Trilogy: The Business Model: Using The Language of Work To Organize and Align Work, Bellingham, WA: Performance International, www.performanceinternational.com.

Langdon, Danny G. and Kathleen Langdon. (2018) The Work Trilogy: The Managing Model: Using The Language of Work To Facilitate Work, Bellingham, WA: Performance International, www.performanceinternational.com.

Langdon, Danny G. and Kathleen Langdon. (2018) The Work Trilogy: The Working Model: Using The Language of Work To Implement Work, Bellingham, WA: Performance International, www.performanceinternational.com.

LoW Books, Articles, YouTube, and Case Studies

Books

Langdon, Danny G. (1995) *The New Language of Work*. Amherst, MA: HRD Press.

Langdon, Danny G. (2000) *Aligning performance: Improving people, systems and organizations*. San Francisco, CA: Jossey-Bass/Pheiffer Publishers.

Langdon, Danny G., Kathleen Whiteside, and Monica McKenna. (1999). *Interventions Resource Guide: 50 Performance Improvement Tools*. San Francisco, CA: Jossey-Bass/Pheiffer Publishers.

Langdon, Danny G., Kathleen Langdon, Johnilee Whiteside, (2014) *Righting the Enterprise – A Primer for Organizing or Reorganizing the Right Way*. Bellingham, WA: Performance International (free from our website) at: http://lnkd.in/d66wnjb or in other formats at: https://www.smashwords.com/books/view/431840

Langdon, Danny G. and Kathleen Langdon. (2018) *The Work Trilogy: The Managing Model: Using The Language of Work To Facilitate Work*, Bellingham, WA: Performance International, www.performanceinternational.com.

Langdon, Danny G. and Kathleen Langdon. (2018) *The Work Trilogy: The Working Model: Using The Language of Work To Implement Work*, Bellingham, WA: Performance International, www.performanceinternational.com.

LoW Related Articles

Langdon, D.G. A new language of work, Quality Digest, Oct., 1994 44-48.

Langdon, D.G. Aligning performance: the ultimate goal of our profession, Performance Improvement Journal, vol. 39, no. 3, 22-26.

Langdon, D.G. Redefining jobs and work in changing organizations, HR Magazine, May, 1996, 97-101.

Langdon, D.G. Return of the craftsman, Unpublished article, available from Performance International.

Langdon, D.G. Self-directed TQM, Unpublished article, available from Performance International..

Langdon, D.G. and Anne F. Marrelli. A new model for systemic competency identification, ISPI Journal, vol. 41, no. 4, 14-21.

Langdon, D.G. reOrganizing your department in 9 steps, Concept Paper, available from Performance International.

Langdon, D.G. Improving management communication through job models, ISPI Journal, vol. 55, no. 7, 17-18.

LoW YouTube Sources

10-Minute Teach: https://youtu.be/Nn7tLm4nRLU

Business Optimization Dashboard: http://www.youtube.com/watch?v=WhS2KMdHm70

YouTube Chats on the Language of Work:

Title	URL
Introduction: Conversations with the Model Maker	https://youtu.be/n8_qrI4S8iQ
Historical Context	https://youtu.be/eToNViGfRqQ
Why Did You Create the Language of Work?	https://youtu.be/mhTXUaZsel4
Essential Elements of Work: Formula Models	https://youtu.be/eRwpkM0VoBk
Work Formula	https://youtu.be/pjmudw2iojY
Work as a System	https://youtu.be/hFpjgo9KuJs
Use of Language of Work for Individuals (Job Model)	https://youtu.bc/GBNczPhNxgU
Language of Work and Reorganizations	https://youtu.be/wvzrzed-pVc
Who Does What in Job Modeling?	https://youtu.be/kJ0o8-6ASXc
Why Two Facilitators?	https://youtu.be/pewSTjet1yM
Skills of Data Gatherer in LOW	https://youtu.be/b_gmbwScdgl
Why Not Brainstorm?	https://youtu.be/OeLSoLOQ4xw
Resistance to Language of Work	https://youtu.be/h_CJorkC6rI
Interface with Human Resources	https://youtu.be/wChyHGHg2wU
Handling Resistance	https://youtu.be/paKRrBHr4Xk
Finite Set of Data for Organizational Development	https://youtu.be/7lckhpbSfic
Improve Organizational Development Practice	https://youtu.be/7YR-4iB25lo

LoW Related Case Studies

Case Studies are available from PerformanceInternational.com and demonstrate various applications of the Language of Work Model:

AQUA Company—Reorganization

The Information Technology (IT) Department at a major water utility had grown like topsy-turvy over a ten-year period, losing credibility with clients and senior management because of its expensive inability to deliver on a promise to develop its own enterprise-wide software. In desperation, after spending many millions of dollars on a non-deliverable, senior management purchased and installed a commercial ERP (SAP) software package. A unit was created to tailor and install the new software, which did not report to the centralized IT department.

A survey showed that 250 people performed IT functions within AQUA, but fewer than 100 reported to the centralized IT unit. The others were spread over several operating departments, and the SAP unit. In other words, like many organizations today, IT was both centralized and decentralized. Senior management wanted to know whether this was the optimal organizational structure; if not, why not, and how any new, proposed structure would compare to other similar companies.

College Student-Centric Studies— Organizational Alignment

A junior college in the Midwest (U.S.) had completed a reorganization (not using the Language of Work model) to reduce the number of administrators, to enhance the registration and financial aid processes, and to reduce personnel costs. The primary goals of the consolidation were to result in increased enrollment, higher student achievement and improved reputation of the college. Once the cuts had been made, it became clear that additional work was needed to understand operationally (a core process) how to achieve goals of being student-centric. It was also clear that the jobs within the new department would also need to change. Specifically, they needed to develop a student-centered process, creating an improved flow for students (including single-stop registration) and enhanced productivity of staff. Finally, improved communication between and among faculty, Student Services staff and students was critical in solving problems and removing obstacles for students to continue school to graduate and increase enrollment.

Defense Contractor— Changing a Corporate Strategy

A great challenge occurs when an enterprise decides, for very good business reasons, to change the strategy it has pursued for years, perhaps since its inception. Ideas are great, and strategic planning sessions are exciting and invigorating. However, it is when the operational aspects of a new strategy must be planned, changed, recruited and trained for seamlessly that trouble can begin. This case study shows a systematic way of translating strategy into operational excellence using the Language of Work Model.

Government Case Study—Culture Change

A government agency outsourced operations and revenue collection to a private company. It became clear that parties on both sides had experienced frustration with the "way things are." Executives in both organizations came to realize that the different cultures of the two organizations had interfered with optimal performance. Both parties wanted to ensure the future relationship would be a model for privatization contracts across North America. A cultural audit would provide the data, analysis and recommendations to help employees of both organizations understand the other and achieve high performance standards.

Hi Tech Case Study—Core Process Improvement

The ability of any organization to protect its employees and its intellectual property from hackers is vital today. The Language of Work™ model for reorganizing allowed this unit to look at all the technical aspects of ensuring IT security while keeping a clear eye on how to get the work done, and aligning the organization's jobs to its core work.

Life Insurance Case Study—Cultural Change

After years of poor management, a new president took over a division of a large insurance company which was losing market share and profitability. He knew he had a short honeymoon period in which to turn the organization around. He selected the authors to aid him because they had a good performance (work) improvement model and could work at all the levels of the organization. They worked closely with him and his management team to define the current and desired state of the business unit, the core processes, the individual jobs, and the work groups—completing all the performance improvement in sixty days.

Major Utility Case Study—
Core Process to Jobs Improvement

The change in weather patterns is placing extreme demands on the utilities and fire departments around the US. An autumn fifty-year snowstorm that followed a devastating hurricane just sixty days earlier caused so much damage that residents and businesses were without electricity for as many as twelve days. The utility was forced to analyze and repair its emergency management system. Analysis using the LoW process model allowed 25 different agencies to develop a coordinated plan to respond to future emergencies.

New Enterprise—New Global Business Formation

The author of this case study is a user of the Language of Work in a global startup. He points to the multiple uses he has made of the LoW model, capturing the essence of the performance aspect of the model. The author can thus see and align the many organizations he is creating because the LoW mirrors what the work of the business will be. He has been "testing" the claims and value of the Language of Work by using it in multiple real-life settings.

Nursing Services—Nonprofit Problem Solving

A nonprofit organization had a new executive director. The agency provided nursing support in homes and in jails, as well as light housekeeping for certain clients. She was aware of myriad financial, reputational and performance problems in the organization she was heading but needed a path for resolving them. By using the LoW AS IS/TO BE Work Analytic Tool, a series of actionable steps were captured for making needed work and cultural changes.

Author Biographies

Danny G. Langdon, Co-founder of Performance International, with forty+ years' experience, has published twelve books, and served as the series editor of the 40-volume "Instructional Designs Library." He is the recipient of three major ISPI awards of excellence, a past international president, and Honorary Life Member. He is the originator of the Language of Work Model,™ and has presented at more than 35 international conferences, published numerous articles, and conducted numerous workshops.

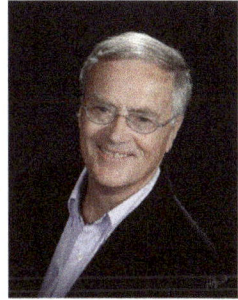

Kathleen Langdon, Co-founder of Performance International, has served external clients for more than thirty years, concentrating on embedding work performance improvement in numerous companies. She served as Corporate Director of Human Resources for a major service medical organization. She is a past president of ISPI, invited speaker for the annual ISPI Awards Banquet, and led 15 business executives to explain performance technology to the White House. She is the co-editor of "Intervention Resource Guide: 50 Performance Improvement Tools," published numerous articles, and is a frequent presenter at conferences here and abroad.

www.ingramcontent.com/pod-product-compliance
Lightning Source LLC
Chambersburg PA
CBHW050730030426
42336CB00012B/1499